Walking The Stranger Road

Forty Daily Reflections

Stephen Cook

Photographs by

Michal Brandstatter

1

Introduction

These short reflections are taken from hundreds written over twenty years of ministry in rural Devon.

They are offered here in a slightly expanded form for daily personal devotions.

They are intended to be read SLOWLY.

It is most important to read the Bible passage given, even if you think you know it, before the reflection.

All Bible passages are taken from the *World English Bible*.

The "Think" section contains suggestions for quiet contemplation. If you don't find them helpful, ask yourself some other questions, but please take some time before moving on to the prayer.

The prayers are deliberately personal and designed to be spoken slowly, one line at a time. They can, of course, be combined with other prayers, as you bring to God the matters of the day and the concerns of your heart.

The photographs are to be used to inspire further prayer, meditation, reflection and contemplation. Notice how you respond to them - in relation to the accompanying text, but also instinctively, organically.

How do they make you feel? What do they make you think? Which do you like more? Why?

Please feel free to write notes and annotate, as directed and guided by your deepest responses - and the Holy Spirit!

Stephen Cook, Michal Brandstatter, February, 2023

When he had sat down at the table with them, he took the bread and gave thanks. Breaking it, he gave it to them. Their eyes were opened and they recognised him, then he vanished out of their sight. They said to one another, "Weren't our hearts burning within us, while he spoke to us along the way, and while he opened the Scriptures to us?"

Luke 24:30-32

Being therefore justified by faith, we have peace with God through our Lord Jesus Christ; through whom we also have our access by faith into this grace in which we stand. We rejoice in hope of the glory of God. Not only this, but we also rejoice in our sufferings, knowing that suffering produces perseverance; and perseverance, proven character; and proven character, hope: and hope doesn't disappoint us, because God's love has been poured into our hearts through the Holy Spirit who was given to us. For while we were yet weak, at the right time Christ died for the ungodly. For one will hardly die for a righteous man. Yet perhaps for a good person someone would even dare to die. But God commends his own love toward us, in that while we were yet sinners, Christ died for us.

Much more then, being now justified by his blood, we will be saved from God's wrath through him. For if while we were enemies, we were reconciled to God through the death of his Son, much more, being reconciled, we will be saved by his life.

Romans 5:1-10

Day One: While We Were Still Sinners

"God shows his love for us in this: while we were still sinners, Christ died for us." We are so used to the idea that Jesus died for us that it is easy to miss the impact of that statement. Most of the religious experience of human beings has involved us sacrificing things to God. We recognise that we have done wrong, and that God (or the gods) may be angry, and we try to make amends. The whole system of religion at the time this was written was based around that idea. Yet here is Jesus turning religion on its head and offering himself for the ungodly.

This is the radical insight of the Christian Faith. God does not wait for us to reach out: God reaches out for us. There are no preconditions, no standard that must be achieved, no ceremony that must be performed, no sacrifice that must be made. While we were still sinners Christ died for us.

That is because the underlying motivation is not justice but love. It was fundamentally unjust that Jesus should die for us: he did not deserve it and we did. This is justice turned backwards. But, out of love for us, God in Jesus took the consequences of justice on himself. It is humbling and liberating to know that the conditions have been met without any preconditions. Christ has already died for us: while we are still sinners.

Think:

- *Do you feel you need to sacrifice for God? Is that a right feeling?*
- *Can you take on board the idea that Jesus died for you?*
- *Can you accept that there are no preconditions?*

Pray:

Lord God,
You do not wait for me to be righteous,
You do not even wait for me to be good,
You accept me, sinner that I am.
I set aside all that I am motivated to sacrifice
In order to earn my salvation,
And instead I accept your sacrifice made once for all.
There is nothing I can offer,
Nothing I can pay,
Nothing I can do
Because it is already finished: already done.
This is how you show your love:
While I was still a sinner Christ died
For me.

At The Door: The Holy Sepulchre, Jerusalem, 2007

"I have many things to speak and to judge concerning you. However he who sent me is true; and the things which I heard from him, these I say to the world."

They didn't understand that he spoke to them about the Father. Jesus therefore said to them, "When you have lifted up the Son of Man, then you will know that I am he, and I do nothing of myself, but as my Father taught me, I say these things. He who sent me is with me. The Father hasn't left me alone, for I always do the things that are pleasing to him."

As he spoke these things, many believed in him. Jesus therefore said to those Jews who had believed him, "If you remain in my word, then you are truly my disciples. You will know the truth, and the truth will make you free."

John 8:26-32

Day Two: Finding Truth, Being Free

How open minded are you? Anyone who has experienced the joys of Facebook may have been drawn into answering various "quizzes" that supposedly reveal something about your character. If you were devising one to test open mindedness, what questions would you ask? Perhaps you would present people with various scenarios and ask for a reaction. But the more I think about it, the more difficult it becomes.

Open mindedness is seen as a virtue: no-one would like to be described as closed minded, but gullibility or indifference, which could bring about the same results, would be seen as bad. Where does open mindedness cross the border into woolly thinking or worse? Perhaps Oliver Cromwell hit the mark in his colourful and much quoted comment to the General Assembly of the Church of Scotland: "I beseech you in the bowels of Christ, think it possible that you may be mistaken," he urged.

To know what you think while at the same time being open to the possibility you may be wrong is the basis of rational argument, and to abandon that idea is the root of all prejudice. Closing our minds to people and ideas can be a defence mechanism: it is disturbing to think we might be wrong, but it also shuts us off from the truth. "You will know the truth and the truth will set you free," Jesus promised. Are you willing to open your mind to the possibility that you may be wrong and look for that liberating truth? You might surprise yourself.

Think:

- *Are there some things you refuse to think about? Why?*
- *When was the last time you changed your mind about something important?*
- *Do you find the idea of knowing the truth about yourself exciting or scary or both?*
- *Pilate asked Jesus, "What is truth?" but didn't wait for an answer. What might the answer have been? What would you have said?*

Pray:

Lord Jesus,
You promised that the truth would set me free.
Free from prejudice,
Free from false thinking,
Free from unhealthy fantasy.
Lord Jesus, I want to know the truth.
I want to be set free.
So I accept I may be wrong
And I open myself to all you want to say to me.
Speak to me this day,
Show me what is true and what is false
So I will know your liberation.

Fly Free: Eastbourne, Sussex, 2022

The third day, there was a wedding in Cana of Galilee. Jesus' mother was there. Jesus also was invited, with his disciples, to the wedding. When the wine ran out, Jesus' mother said to him, "They have no wine." Jesus said to her, "Woman, what does that have to do with you and me? My hour has not yet come."His mother said to the servants, "Whatever he says to you, do it." Now there were six water pots of stone set there after the Jews' way of purifying, containing two or three metretes apiece. Jesus said to them, "Fill the water pots with water." So they filled them up to the brim. He said to them, "Now draw some out, and take it to the ruler of the feast." So they took it. When the ruler of the feast tasted the water now become wine, and didn't know where it came from (but the servants who had drawn the water knew), the ruler of the feast called the bridegroom and said to him, "Everyone serves the good wine first, and when the guests have drunk freely, then that which is worse. You have kept the good wine until now!" This beginning of his signs Jesus did in Cana of Galilee, and revealed his glory; and his disciples believed in him.

John 2:1-11

Day Three: All The Longings Of Our Hearts

The first part of John's Gospel is arranged differently to the others. There are a series of "signs", often followed by a section of teaching, revealing something about Jesus and what he had come to do. John ends the story of the turning of water into wine by saying "Jesus did this, the first of his signs… and revealed his glory; and his disciples believed in him." What does it say about God that the first miracle his Son performed was the turning of 180 gallons of water into the very best quality wine? How does that match the idea of the kill-joy, fun-hating God who is only out to condemn us, that people think we believe in?

Jesus did this out of compassion. The wine had run out, which for the bride and groom would have been a major embarrassment. No-one would have died, but the guests would have gone home sober, and they would have remembered the wedding where there was not enough wine. Mary and Jesus are sensitive even to this low-level disaster. God cares, even about things as trivial as this. The bridegroom's disgrace was turned into honour and, we might imagine, the guests had a very good time.

I went to Cana a while ago. You won't be surprised when I tell you that you can buy wine there. I am sure if you ask the merchants, they will say it is part of the original batch. It is typical of Jesus' miracles that he not only helped a couple at a wedding but ensured an income for the village ever after. No wonder his disciples believed in him.

Think:

- Does your image of God match what you see in this miracle?
- Are there small areas of concern in your life you have not brought to God because you feel they are too trivial?
- Could you be like Mary, and bring to God the impending disasters you can see in other peoples' lives?
- What's the equivalent of the "best wine" that you would like to ask God for?

Pray:

Gracious God,
You know the longings of my heart.
You long to give me the very best.
But I am slow to ask,
And often think my needs are not your concern.
You are the guest in my house
But I do not acknowledge your presence.
Please take my fear of looking bad in the eyes of others;
My fear of looking mean.
Please take the little that I have and turn it into abundance
As you did at that wedding so long ago.
May I see the miracle of transformation
And believe in you.

Waiting: Mill End Hotel, Chagford, 2016

Again he began to teach by the seaside. A great multitude was gathered to him, so that he entered into a boat in the sea, and sat down. All the multitude were on the land by the sea. He taught them many things in parables, and told them in his teaching, "Listen! Behold, the farmer went out to sow, and as he sowed, some seed fell by the road, and the birds came and devoured it. Others fell on the rocky ground, where it had little soil, and immediately it sprang up, because it had no depth of soil. When the sun had risen, it was scorched; and because it had no root, it withered away. Others fell among the thorns, and the thorns grew up, and choked it, and it yielded no fruit. Others fell into the good ground, and yielded fruit, growing up and increasing. Some produced thirty times, some sixty times, and some one hundred times as much." He said, "Whoever has ears to hear, let him hear." When he was alone, those who were around him with the twelve asked him about the parables. He said to them, "To you is given the mystery of God's Kingdom, but to those who are outside, all things are done in parables."

Mark 14:1-11

Day Four: Extravagant Worship

The first church I was responsible for as a vicar was a multi-purpose building on a council estate. It had a panel of frosted glass on one wall: over the years, various panes had been broken and replaced, always with a slightly different pattern, so that the overall effect was, well, less than beautiful. Wanting to make the place more special, we devised a scheme to replace the window with modern stained glass. We found a local designer and held a church meeting to discuss it.

There were some concerns, but the general feeling was favourable, until one church member stood up to speak. "I cannot support spending this amount of money on stained glass when there are millions of starving people in the world," he said. There were nods around the room: the moral high ground had been taken. We agreed to think more but the stained glass never happened (nor did we give the money to the poor, I might add).

The disciples objected to the woman using expensive perfume to anoint Jesus' feet: the money could have gone to the poor, they said. "You will always have the poor," said Jesus, "You will not always have me." All worship is an extravagance: we could spend our time doing so many more useful things, but, as we offer beautiful things to God, so we become more beautiful and, wonderfully, the poor are fed as well.

Think:

- *Why did the disciples react in this way? Might you have done the same?*
- *What holds you back from being extravagant in your worship?*
- *Is there something you have been saving that you could offer to God?*
- *What did Jesus mean when he said, "You will always have the poor, but you will not always have me?"*

Pray:

Lord Jesus,
My worship of you is often poor and restrained.
I don't give you the honour you deserve
because I am keeping it for myself.
I want to break open the jar and pour it out,
I want to kneel at your feet,
but I am concerned about what others may think.
So I give you what I have:
The things I have been saving,
The things I have been afraid to lose.
As you accepted the worship of that woman
Accept my own sinful self
And by your grace may the poor be fed as well.

Extravagant: Abbey House, Glastonbury, 2016

19

"You are the salt of the earth, but if the salt has lost its flavour, with what will it be salted? It is then good for nothing, but to be cast out and trodden under the feet of men. You are the light of the world. A city located on a hill can't be hidden. Neither do you light a lamp and put it under a measuring basket, but on a stand; and it shines to all who are in the house. Even so, let your light shine before men, that they may see your good works and glorify your Father who is in heaven."

Matthew 5:13-16

Day Five: Holy In The Everyday

Two catholic priests, who were both heavy smokers, had an audience with the Pope. The first went in and after a while he said, "Holy Father, there is something which is troubling me. Is it OK to smoke while I'm praying?" The Pope frowned and told him that would not be appropriate: it would be disrespectful and dishonouring to God. The priest came out looking downcast, knowing it would be very hard for him to keep this rule. The second priest, seeing his friend's face, thought for a few moments then went in to see the Pope. "Holy Father," he said, "I've been thinking: is it OK to pray while I'm smoking?"

There is something quite profound about that story. One question was about allowing the world to intrude into God's territory and the other is about allowing God to intrude on the world's territory. One is always a bad thing, the other always good.

It would be wrong to smoke in church, just as it would be to text or read a book or do your make-up, but there is no reason at all why you should not turn any activity into an opportunity for prayer. You wouldn't chat to a friend while praying, but there is no reason not to pray while you are chatting to a friend. We can take the ordinary activities of life and hallow them by offering them up to God.

Think:

- *Do you let God into your everyday life?*
- *Are there ways in which your everyday life intrudes into your relationship with God?*
- *What does it mean to be the salt of the earth?*
- *What does it mean to be the light of the world?*
- *How are the passage and the story connected?*

Pray:

Thank you, Lord God
That you have made me salt and light.
I don't have to become salt and light:
I already am.
I just need to be salt for the earth
And to let my light shine.
Shine in me and through me:
Make the everyday holy
And bless the ordinary with your presence.
May I be holy, as you are holy.

Shining Bright: Plymouth Aquarium, Devon, 2021

Owe no one anything, except to love one another; for he who loves his neighbour has fulfilled the law. For the commandments, "You shall not commit adultery," "You shall not murder," "You shall not steal," "You shall not covet," and whatever other commandments there are, are all summed up in this saying, namely, "You shall love your neighbour as yourself." Love doesn't harm a neighbour. Love therefore is the fulfilment of the law.

Romans 13:8-10

Day Six: It's About Love

I am always suspicious when someone tells me "The Bible says" something, just as I am when a tabloid newspaper tells me that "scientists say" something or "experts agree" something. When did experts ever agree about anything? The Bible is a library of books written over centuries and working out what it "says" is rarely simple.

But in our passage, St Paul, quoting Jesus, gives us a compass to guide us through the complex landscape of the Bible's teaching about right and wrong. All laws, he tells us, derive their authority from the great laws: to love God and to love your neighbour as yourself. If you keep these two you will automatically keep all the others.

So there is a hierarchy of law in the Bible. Some teachings are more important than others. Some are fundamental, some are derivative. If we want to understand anything the Bible says about right and wrong, we must do so in the light of the overriding law of love. We must ask, "How does this part of what the Bible says relate to the great commandments?" All moral decisions are ultimately about finding the most loving course of action. If it isn't about loving God or your neighbour, then the Bible doesn't "say" it at all. That's what the Bible says.

Think:

- Which of the Ten Commandments do you find hardest to keep?
- How are those commandments related to the great commands?
- What needs to change if you are to keep those commands?
- What would you like to ask God for in this regard?

Pray:

Lord God,
You command us to love you with all our heart, mind soul and strength
And to love our neighbour as ourselves.
This is too hard for me.
But I know that to please you I don't need to try harder:
I need to love more.
Please help me to know your love that passes knowledge
And to be filled with your fullness,
So that loving you is easy
And loving my neighbour follows on.
I ask this in the name of him, who through his great love
Died and rose again:
Jesus Christ, my Lord.

Two Girls: Clefmont, France, 2016

Now faith is assurance of things hoped for, proof of things not seen. For, by this, the elders obtained testimony. By faith, we understand that the universe has been framed by the word of God, so that what is seen has not been made out of things which are visible …

By faith, Abraham, when he was called, obeyed to go out to the place which he was to receive for an inheritance. He went out, not knowing where he went. By faith, he lived as an alien in the land of promise, as in a land not his own, dwelling in tents with Isaac and Jacob, the heirs with him of the same promise. For he looked for the city which has the foundations, whose builder and maker is God.

By faith, even Sarah herself received power to conceive, and she bore a child when she was past age, since she counted him faithful who had promised. Therefore as many as the stars of the sky in multitude, and as innumerable as the sand which is by the sea shore, were fathered by one man, and him as good as dead.

These all died in faith, not having received the promises, but having seen them and embraced them from afar, and having confessed that they were strangers and pilgrims on the earth. For those who say such things make it clear that they are seeking a country of their own. If indeed they had been thinking of that country from which they went out, they would have had enough time to return. But now they desire a better country, that is, a heavenly one. Therefore God is not ashamed of them, to be called their God, for he has prepared a city for them.

Hebrews 11:1-3; 8-16

Day Seven: Trusting God

We tend to make very big decisions based on very little evidence. We might decide to buy a house, for example, on the basis that it "feels right", rather than the distance from the shops or the size of the garage. When it comes to the biggest decision we will ever make: the choice of who to marry, we will undoubtedly know a lot about our future partner before the big day, but there will be a lot we don't know as well. Hiring a private detective to investigate their past relationships, or asking them to undergo a psychometric test to see if you are compatible would not be a good idea: they might well say, "I thought you loved me: don't you trust me?"

"Now faith is the assurance of things hoped for: the conviction of things not seen," says the writer to the Hebrews. He goes on to list great heroes of faith, starting with Abraham, who, against all the odds, believed God when he was told he would be the father of a great nation. To believe with no evidence is foolish, but proof and faith are not compatible. Evidence is the foundation for faith, but it cannot be the whole building: in the end faith is a decision to trust.

I could give you some reasons to believe in God but if you were to ask me why I believe I would tell you a story: the story of how at each stage of my life, as I have decided to trust, God has proved trustworthy. That is the nature of faith: from the starting point of what we know, we step out into what we cannot know and find ourselves on the firm ground of God's trustworthiness.

Think:

- *Looking back at big decisions you have made, which ones have involved the most faith?*
- *On reflection, have there been times when you should have trusted God more?*
- *Are there decisions you are reserving for yourself which you know you should trust to God?*
- *What are your barriers when it comes to assurance and conviction?*

Pray:

God of Abraham,
You call me to trust you
For a future I cannot see.
You ask me to believe in what seems to be impossible.
Yet my heart tells me that you are faithful
And that you want even more for me than I want for myself.
So I reach out my hand
And place it in yours.
Where you lead, I will follow,
What you command I will do
Until I reach that better country:
The heavenly city you have prepared for me.

Southgate Madonna: Buckfast Abbey, Devon, 2015

Let as many as are bondservants under the yoke count their own masters worthy of all honour, that the name of God and the doctrine not be blasphemed. Those who have believing masters, let them not despise them because they are brothers, but rather let them serve them, because those who partake of the benefit are believing and beloved. Teach and exhort these things.

If anyone teaches a different doctrine, and doesn't consent to sound words, the words of our Lord Jesus Christ, and to the doctrine which is according to godliness, he is conceited, knowing nothing, but obsessed with arguments, disputes, and word battles, from which come envy, strife, insulting, evil suspicions, constant friction of people of corrupt minds and destitute of the truth, who suppose that godliness is a means of gain. Withdraw yourself from such.

But godliness with contentment is great gain. For we brought nothing into the world, and we certainly can't carry anything out. But having food and clothing, we will be content with that. But those who are determined to be rich fall into a temptation, a snare, and many foolish and harmful lusts, such as drown men in ruin and destruction. For the love of money is a root of all kinds of evil. Some have been led astray from the faith in their greed, and have pierced themselves through with many sorrows.

Timothy 6:1-10

Day Eight: Godliness With Contentment

"There is great gain in godliness combined with contentment," says the writer to Timothy. Contentment is different to complacency. Complacency is refusing to recognise what needs to change. Contentment is appreciating what does not need to change. As the saying goes, "Happiness is not about having what you want, it is about wanting what you have."

The passage continues with words sometimes read at funerals: "We brought nothing into the world, and we take nothing out... as long as we have enough for our daily needs, we will be satisfied with that." The world system feeds on our discontent. Are our teeth clean enough? Is our house big enough? Is our family as happy as the one pictured? Am I a good parent? Am I handsome / successful / sweet-smelling? The list goes on.

Contentment needs to be combined with godliness. Godliness for the Christian is about modelling our life on Jesus. Can you imagine Jesus being concerned about what car he drove or how white his teeth were? Discontent is modelled on a false image of true humanity. A concern for godliness presents us with a different understanding of what it means to be fully human based on the one person who is fully human. That is why a combination of godliness and contentment brings great gain.

Think:

- *What are the main sources of discontent in your life at the moment?*
- *What are the main sources of contentment?*
- *Is your ambition for yourself based on a world view of what it means to be human or on Jesus?*
- *What does "godliness" mean to you? What would be the gains?*

Pray:

Lord Jesus,
I want to be like you:
To model my life on yours,
So that what I want is what you want,
What I love is what you love
And what I hate is what you hate.
I want to grow up in every way into you.
Please open my eyes so that I can see
how I have been deceived
into the world's way of thinking.
Help me to understand my discontent
And to know that godliness and contentment
Bring great gain.

La Petite Marie: Fresnes-Sur-Apance, France, 2022

Then Peter came and said to him, "Lord, how often shall my brother sin against me, and I forgive him? Until seven times?"

Jesus said to him, "I don't tell you until seven times, but, until seventy times seven. Therefore the Kingdom of Heaven is like a certain king, who wanted to settle accounts with his servants. When he had begun to settle, one was brought to him who owed him ten thousand talents. But because he couldn't pay, his lord commanded him to be sold, with his wife, his children, and all that he had, and payment to be made. The servant therefore fell down and knelt before him, saying, 'Lord, have patience with me, and I will repay you all!' The lord of that servant, being moved with compassion, released him and forgave him the debt.

"But that servant went out and found one of his fellow servants who owed him one hundred denarii,[b] and he grabbed him and took him by the throat, saying, 'Pay me what you owe!'

"So his fellow servant fell down at his feet and begged him, saying, 'Have patience with me, and I will repay you!' He would not, but went and cast him into prison until he should pay back that which was due. So when his fellow servants saw what was done, they were exceedingly sorry, and came and told their lord all that was done. Then his lord called him in and said to him, 'You wicked servant! I forgave you all that debt because you begged me. Shouldn't you also have had mercy on your fellow servant, even as I had mercy on you?' His lord was angry, and delivered him to the tormentors until he should pay all that was due to him. So my heavenly Father will also do to you, if you don't each forgive your brother from your hearts for his misdeeds."

Matthew 18:21-35

Day Nine: Forgiveness

When the subject of Christian forgiveness is talked about, people often jump to the big scenarios. "You mean if someone killed all of my family, I would be supposed to forgive them?" Amazingly, there are some very moving stories of people who have somehow found the strength to do just that, but it is hard for most of us to imagine being able to do anything of the kind. Fortunately that is most unlikely to be asked of us.

Jesus told the parable of the unforgiving servant: the man who was forgiven a huge debt but refused to forgive a small one, as a result of which he came to a sticky end. It is important to notice that the question which led to the story was not about how much we should forgive but how often, and the story itself is about the failure to forgive a small debt, not a big one.

So the parable encourages us to start with the small things we need to forgive, and the things we need to forgive often. We need to let go of the little things: the ways in which other people don't do what they said they would or disappoint, irritate and frustrate us. We need to learn to forgive the minor insensitivities and slights, the sense of being passed over or ignored, the petty acts of selfishness or ignorance we encounter every day. If we can start with these small things, maybe in time we can learn how to forgive the bigger things as well.

Think:

- *Are you naturally a forgiving person?*
- *Do you have a strong sense of being forgiven by God?*
- *Are there any small "debts" you are holding on to that you should let go of?*
- *What one thing could you do today to take this parable seriously?*

Pray:

Heavenly Father,
You command me to forgive others their trespasses,
As you have forgiven me.
I give you the small things that have been done to me:
The ways in which I have been made to feel bad.
Please help me to see these in the light of my own forgiveness
And to understand how trivial they are when set beside the cross.
Please set me free from the desire for revenge,
So that I exchange cursing for blessing,
And justice for mercy.
I ask in the name of your Son,
Who died so that
I might have forgiveness:
Jesus Christ, my Lord.

Open Door: Grignoncourt, France, 2022

But concerning the times and the seasons, brothers, you have no need that anything be written to you. For you yourselves know well that the day of the Lord comes like a thief in the night. For when they are saying, "Peace and safety," then sudden destruction will come on them, like birth pains on a pregnant woman. Then they will in no way escape. But you, brothers, aren't in darkness, that the day should overtake you like a thief. You are all children of light and children of the day. We don't belong to the night, nor to darkness, so then let's not sleep, as the rest do, but let's watch and be sober. For those who sleep, sleep in the night; and those who are drunk are drunk in the night. But since we belong to the day, let's be sober, putting on the breastplate of faith and love, and for a helmet, the hope of salvation. For God didn't appoint us to wrath, but to the obtaining of salvation through our Lord Jesus Christ, who died for us, that, whether we wake or sleep, we should live together with him. Therefore exhort one another, and build each other up, even as you also do.

1 Thessalonians 5:1-11

Day Ten: Being Sober, Being Brave

The word "sober" comes twice in two sentences in this passage from the letter to the Thessalonians. Misuse of alcohol was as much of a problem in the 1st century as it is now, but the word is used to mean more than not being drunk. Just as we use "sober" to mean serious and reflective, so does Paul. When we think about ourselves and about the future of the world we should do so in a sober manner.

People have always used alcohol as a means of escaping reality. While the effects last you can lose your inhibitions, believe your jokes are funny and that you really, really love your best mate who you've only just met. But there are plenty of other ways of escaping reality, the most effective of which is just refusing to think about it, filling our lives with sugar and fluff and focussing on the trivial.

It is important to think about the world and about ourselves with sober judgement. We can't do it all the time, but we can do it sometimes. We can take stock, we can ask hard questions and expect straight answers from ourselves about whether our priorities are right, whether our deeds match our words, and whether we are heading in the right direction. Every so often we need to stop hiding from reality and dare to face up to it. It's in that context that we can enjoy life to the full, as God intends.

Think:

- What are your mechanisms for hiding from reality?
- Are you using them in a healthy way?
- The passage offers some alternative ways of shielding ourselves: what do they mean?
- What might being more "awake" and "sober" mean for you?

Pray:

Lord God,
You see me; I cannot hide from you.
I want to face reality with sober judgement
But I am afraid of what I will find,
I am afraid it will be too much too bear.
I know you are beside me now
And that you will be with me as the future unfolds.
So I set aside the false armour,
And put on faith and love as a breastplate,
And the hope of salvation as a helmet,
And I step forward to face this day
With honesty and courage,
To be your person in this place.

Bright Courage: Sampford Peverell, Devon, 2022

"You have heard that it was said to the ancient ones, 'You shall not murder;' and 'Whoever murders will be in danger of the judgment.' But I tell you that everyone who is angry with his brother without a cause will be in danger of the judgment. Whoever says to his brother, 'Raca!' will be in danger of the council. Whoever says, 'You fool!' will be in danger of the fire of Gehenna.

"If therefore you are offering your gift at the altar, and there remember that your brother has anything against you, leave your gift there before the altar, and go your way. First be reconciled to your brother, and then come and offer your gift. Agree with your adversary quickly while you are with him on the way; lest perhaps the prosecutor deliver you to the judge, and the judge deliver you to the officer, and you be cast into prison. Most certainly I tell you, you shall by no means get out of there until you have paid the last penny.

Matthew 5:21-26

Day Eleven: Being Peacemakers

We all get angry sometimes. Occasionally our anger is justified; most often it is just because things have not gone the way we want them to. There is a lot of anger around, and it can find its way into church life. There were famous fallings out between people in the Bible and they have been repeated throughout church history. It is very sad and very damaging when a Christian brother or sister cannot agree with another to the point where there is bitterness, even hatred, between them.

Perhaps that is why Jesus, in this passage from the Sermon on the Mount, warns against anger in such strong terms: talking about judgement, even hell fire, for those who are guilty. Instead, he says, we must make peace with our brother or sister before offering our worship to God. Such peace-making is not about a warm cosy feeling, it is about a decision to let go of the offence in the recognition that God has let go of our own offences.

In any case, the person most likely to be hurt by our anger is us. It will become a pool of bitterness if we hold onto it. Letting go of our anger sets us free from its corrosive effects. When we have been badly hurt, that is very hard to do, and we need to come back to the cross, and remember what our own forgiveness cost. We make peace in the name and the style of the great Peace Maker.

Think:

- *What is niggling you at the moment?*
- *Is there anyone you feel angry with?*
- *Where does you anger come from? How justified is it?*
- *Is it possible for you to be a peacemaker?*

Pray:

Lord God,
I don't want to be angry or irritable,
But still it comes out of me,
Unbidden and unwanted.
Sometimes I turn it back on myself
Sometimes I turn it onto others.
Fill me with your spirit so there is no room for this.
Soothe me, sweeten me, calm me,
So that my anger turns into mercy
And I can be a peacemaker.
And be blessed because I am your child.

Sacred Sky: Kingswear, Devon, 2019

"Again you have heard that it was said to the ancient ones, 'You shall not make false vows, but shall perform to the Lord your vows, but I tell you, don't swear at all: neither by heaven, for it is the throne of God; nor by the earth, for it is the footstool of his feet; nor by Jerusalem, for it is the city of the great King. Neither shall you swear by your head, for you can't make one hair white or black. But let your 'Yes' be 'Yes' and your 'No' be 'No.' Whatever is more than these is of the evil one."

Matthew 5:33-37

Day Twelve: Integrity

Having talked about murder, adultery and divorce, Jesus tells his hearers not to swear. In this case he is not talking about bad language, but about the calling down of curses. If someone made a solemn vow, they might name some terrible thing that would happen to them if they should fail to keep it, or they might call on some deity to witness what they were saying and hold them to account if they should prove false. "No," said Jesus. "Just let your yes mean yes and your no mean no. Be the kind of people who keep their promises."

We all make promises every day: "I'll call you back", "We must meet up", "I'll think about it", "I won't let you down", "I'll pray for you". As people of the Word we should be people of our word. If we tell someone we will give something some thought, then we should give it some thought. If we tell someone we will pray for them, we should do so. They may never know that we have done what we said we would, but why would we say something and not do it? Why compromise our integrity with a false promise?

I would like to encourage you to take your small promises seriously. In a way the small ones are more critical because there are no penalties for not keeping them and so they are a bigger test of your character. If you say you will do something: do it. If you know you are not going to do something: say so. Let your 'yes' mean 'yes' and your 'no' mean 'no'.

Think:

- *What small promises have you made in the last few days?*
- *Have you kept them?*
- *What promises have you made to yourself?*
- *What promises have you made to God?*
- *Why do you think keeping promises matters?*

Pray:

God of truth,
You are faithful to your promises:
Help me to be faithful to mine.
I want to be a person of integrity,
Whose 'yes' means 'yes'
And whose 'no' means 'no'.
I pray for those to whom I have made commitments,
Both large and small.
I renew my pledge to be a person of my word
And to do what I have said I would do.
May your faithfulness to me
Be reflected in my faithfulness to others
So that you may be honoured in my actions.
I ask this in the name of the Lord of all faithfulness
Jesus Christ, my Lord.

Two Men: Trafalgar Square, London, 2022

"I am the true vine, and my Father is the farmer. Every branch in me that doesn't bear fruit, he takes away. Every branch that bears fruit, he prunes, that it may bear more fruit. You are already pruned clean because of the word which I have spoken to you. Remain in me, and I in you. As the branch can't bear fruit by itself unless it remains in the vine, so neither can you, unless you remain in me. I am the vine. You are the branches. He who remains in me and I in him bears much fruit, for apart from me you can do nothing. If a man doesn't remain in me, he is thrown out as a branch and is withered; and they gather them, throw them into the fire, and they are burned. If you remain in me, and my words remain in you, you will ask whatever you desire, and it will be done for you. "In this my Father is glorified, that you bear much fruit; and so you will be my disciples."

John 15:1-8

Day Thirteen: Being Pruned

In one of my previous jobs there was a fig tree beside an old country church. Every year it would produce two or three figs. I told the church wardens that we would share them out: one for each of us. Then one day I arrived at church to find that they had decided to prune the tree. It was just a sad looking stem with a few branches sticking out. I was cross: no figs this year. But next time I passed I noticed some buds: the tree had survived. Each Sunday it looked better than the last, until one day I arrived to find it laden with figs: enough for everyone in the congregation.

"My Father is the gardener," said Jesus. "Every branch that bears fruit, he prunes so that it may bear more fruit." The cruel process of pruning produces fruit by focussing the energy of the tree in the right place. In the same way, our lives need pruning of the fruitless growth we produce so that our energy can go into productive places.

You may have experienced God's pruning. I don't mean bad things happening for good reasons, I mean doors closing and others opening, a "no" where we expected a "yes", things being brought to an end, a steer in a new direction. We need to learn to be obedient to the Gardener in these things, trusting that he knows best and wants the best for us. That way our lives can be full of fruit.

Think:

- Are there ways you have experienced positive pruning?
- Are you aware of aspects of your life that still need pruning?
- What kind of fruit do you think the Gardener wants you to produce?

Pray:

Lord Jesus,
You are the vine
And the Father is the gardener.
I know that I need pruning:
I develop in unfruitful ways,
My energy is lost in pointless things.
I want to grow strong and tall and fruitful,
So I submit to your pruning,
Knowing you want the best for me.

Three Colours Leaf: Okehampton, Devon, 2015

55

They came to Jericho. As he went out from Jericho, with his disciples and a great multitude, the son of Timaeus, Bartimaeus, a blind beggar, was sitting by the road. When he heard that it was Jesus the Nazarene, he began to cry out, and say, "Jesus, you son of David, have mercy on me!" Many rebuked him, that he should be quiet, but he cried out much more, "You son of David, have mercy on me!"

Jesus stood still, and said, "Call him." They called the blind man, saying to him, "Cheer up! Get up. He is calling you!"

He, casting away his cloak, sprang up, and came to Jesus.

Jesus asked him, "What do you want me to do for you?" The blind man said to him, "Rabboni, that I may see again."

Jesus said to him, "Go your way. Your faith has made you well." Immediately he received his sight, and followed Jesus on the way.

Mark 10:46-52

Day Fourteen: Asking, Receiving, Healing

The healing of blind Bartimaeus is one of my favourite Bible stories. When he pushes through the crowd, Jesus asks him, "What do you want me to do for you?" You'd think it would be obvious: the man was blind, what else would he want? But we read that into the story because we know what happened. Bartimaeus could have asked for less and maybe he could have asked for more. In the end Jesus says to him, "Go: your faith has made you well."

Several times in the healing miracles, Jesus makes it clear that it is the faith of the asker that has been the active ingredient in the outcome. In fact he often does nothing but declare this to be the case: no touching, no incantations, no prayer to his Heavenly Father, just a pronouncement about what faith has achieved.

Maybe Jesus is asking you that question today: "What do you want me to do for you?" What do you dare to believe? Are you going to ask for a lot, which feels risky, or a little, which feels safer? It takes a lot of soul-searching to find that place of harmony between our desires and God's, but when we find it, we can ask with confidence that we will hear the response, "Go: your faith has made you well."

Think:

- *What would you most like Jesus to do for you?*
- *Are there deeper things you could ask for?*
- *What would being "made well" mean for you?*

Pray:

Lord, you call me to come to you,
And you ask me what I would like you to do for me.
I want to be made well.
I want to be made whole.
I want to be able to see.
I want to follow you in the way.
So I kneel in the dust before you
With my deepest needs
And listen for your voice:
"Go, your faith has made you well."

Alight: Stone Lane Gardens, Devon, 2016

But Thomas, one of the twelve, called Didymus, wasn't with them when Jesus came. The other disciples therefore said to him, "We have seen the Lord!"

But he said to them, "Unless I see in his hands the print of the nails, put my finger into the print of the nails, and put my hand into his side, I will not believe."

After eight days again his disciples were inside and Thomas was with them. Jesus came, the doors being locked, and stood in the middle, and said, "Peace be to you." 27 Then he said to Thomas, "Reach here your finger, and see my hands. Reach here your hand, and put it into my side. Don't be unbelieving, but believing."

Thomas answered him, "My Lord and my God!"

Jesus said to him, "Because you have seen me, you have believed. Blessed are those who have not seen, and have believed." Therefore Jesus did many other signs in the presence of his disciples, which are not written in this book; 31 but these are written, that you may believe that Jesus is the Christ, the Son of God, and that believing you may have life in his name.

John 20:24-31

Day Fifteen: Courage To Believe

Near the end of his Gospel, John reveals his editorial policy: Jesus did many more things that he has not recorded, but these are written down so that you, the reader, may believe, and that, as a result, you might have life. Unlike doubting Thomas, who had to see before he believed, we have only the evidence of the witnesses, carefully presented by John and the others, on which to base our verdict.

There are two kinds of evidence. One is the kind of thing you can do in a laboratory: experiments you can repeat and peer review. No experiment could prove or disprove the hypothesis that Jesus rose from the dead, so we are left with the other kind of evidence: that of witnesses. These were the people who were there, and who often went to martyrs' deaths for what they believed, and the countless people since who in one way or another have encountered the Lord.

One of the most convincing witnesses is the church itself. Why are we still celebrating the life of an obscure Galilean who, at the time of his death, had a tiny band of followers, one of whom betrayed him, and the rest ran away? He wrote no book, founded no institutions, passed no laws. Something happened: something profound and world changing. The gospels have no doubt what that was: Jesus was dead and is alive - and they offer us their testimony so that we might believe, and, believing, we might have life.

Think:

- *Which aspects of faith do you find easy to believe?*
- *What do you find hard to believe?*
- *Can you accept the resurrection as an historical event?*
- *What is the evidence for it?*
- *What's the connection between believing and having life?*

Pray:

Lord, I believe, help my unbelief.
I offer to you the faith I have
And ask you to enable it to grow.
I don't ask to know all the answers,
But for the assurance that the answers
are there to be found.
I believe that Jesus is the Messiah,
The Son of God
And, that because I believe,
I have life in his name.

On This Rock: Sea of Galilee, 2007

So when they had eaten their breakfast, Jesus said to Simon Peter, "Simon, son of Jonah, do you love me more than these?" He said to him, "Yes, Lord; you know that I have affection for you." He said to him, "Feed my lambs."

He said to him again a second time, "Simon, son of Jonah, do you love me?" He said to him, "Yes, Lord; you know that I have affection for you." He said to him, "Tend my sheep."

He said to him the third time, "Simon, son of Jonah, do you have affection for me?"

Peter was grieved because he asked him the third time, "Do you have affection for me?" He said to him, "Lord, you know everything. You know that I have affection for you."

Jesus said to him, "Feed my sheep. Most certainly I tell you, when you were young, you dressed yourself and walked where you wanted to. But when you are old, you will stretch out your hands, and another will dress you and carry you where you don't want to go."

Now he said this, signifying by what kind of death he would glorify God. When he had said this, he said to him, "Follow me."

John 21:15-19

Day Sixteen: Speaking Love, Feeding Sheep

After the resurrection, Jesus asks Peter three times if he loves him. Each time Peter says, "You know that I do." Each time Jesus tells him to "Feed my sheep". Just as Peter had denied Jesus three times, now he goes through this painful process of reinstatement. On the third time he says to Jesus, "Lord you know everything…" If Jesus knows what is in Peter's heart, why does he have to keep asking?

I suppose it is because what we say matters. Peter had denied Jesus with his lips, not his heart: no-one was harmed by what he said, yet afterwards he went out and wept bitterly. The Bible says that if we believe in our hearts and confess with our lips, we will be saved: believing alone is not enough. Peter was the first to declare Jesus to be the Son of God. Now he has denied three times he had ever heard of him, so he has to say three times that he loves him.

It is important to articulate the good things in our hearts and to deny the bad a voice. It is through our speaking that good and evil gain access to the world: we are the door keepers. So we tell the people we love that we love them, we even tell God that we love him, even though God knows all things before we speak. "Tend my sheep" follows naturally. Which is easier: to speak lovingly or to act lovingly? The answer may not be as obvious as it seems. Try speaking first and see what difference it makes.

Think:

- *Can you think of something you now regret saying? Where did that come from?*
- *Are there people you need to tell that you love them?*
- *Are there ways in which you need to speak out the faith that is inside?*
- *How might you do that?*
- *What might "Feed my sheep" mean for you?*

Pray:

Lord, you know all things,
You know that I love you.
I know that my actions don't always match my faith,
And that what I say is not what I believe.
So I say again that I love you.
I am sorry for the times when I have denied you.
I embrace the task and the future you have for me.
Please show me what I must do
To feed your sheep.

Sheep: Dartmoor, Devon, 2022

I exhort therefore, first of all, that petitions, prayers, intercessions, and givings of thanks be made for all men: for kings and all who are in high places, that we may lead a tranquil and quiet life in all godliness and reverence. For this is good and acceptable in the sight of God our Saviour, who desires all people to be saved and come to full knowledge of the truth. For there is one God, and one mediator between God and men, the man Christ Jesus, who gave himself as a ransom for all, the testimony in its own times, to which I was appointed a preacher and an apostle—I am telling the truth in Christ, not lying—a teacher of the Gentiles in faith and truth.

Timothy 2:1-7

Day Seventeen: Praying For Those In Power

Every Sunday in church we pray in one way or another for "those in authority". This is something that the Bible commands us to do, as we have just read. Praying for people with whom we may not agree doesn't come naturally to us, and there is something in the back of our minds which worries we may be endorsing them with our prayers. But, there it is in black and white, and those in charge in Bible times were considerably worse than our own leaders.

There is a lovely phrase in the Prayer Book where we pray for the monarch: "That under him we may be quietly and peaceably governed". The role of those with authority is to hold the ring: to enable the ordinary business of life to go on without conflict or injustice, to create the famous "level playing field" on which everyone has a chance to thrive. Their responsibility is to govern for all the people without fear or prejudice.

For ordinary human beings to do this requires a miracle and that is what we pray for: that somehow people may rise above the power they hold and not be corrupted by it. We ask that they may be surrounded by good advice, that the burden of responsibility may weigh heavy on their shoulders, that they may genuinely seek the good of all and not just of those who put them there. We ask that peace may come to our planet, as those in authority are covered with our prayers.

Think:

- *Who is in authority over you? (Think local, regional, national)*
- *Do you ever pray for them?*
- *What are the barriers?*
- *What would you like to pray for them?*
- *Why do you think it might be important?*

Pray:

Lord God,
There are people with authority over me.
Some of them I like,
Some of them I don't.
You command me to pray for them all and so I will.
I pray for wisdom.
I pray for compassion.
I pray for humility.
I pray for an ability to listen and an ability to decide.
That under them we may be quietly and peaceably governed.
I pray that, whoever is in charge,
My contribution to my society may be positive and helpful
And that I will use the power I have
To govern as I would like to be governed.
In Jesus' name.

Magic Land: Glastonbury, Somerset, 2015

"Don't let your heart be troubled. Believe in God. Believe also in me. In my Father's house are many homes. If it weren't so, I would have told you. I am going to prepare a place for you. If I go and prepare a place for you, I will come again, and will receive you to myself; that where I am, you may be there also. You know where I go, and you know the way." Thomas said to him, "Lord, we don't know where you are going. How can we know the way?" Jesus said to him, "I am the way, the truth, and the life. No one comes to the Father, except through me. If you had known me, you would have known my Father also. From now on, you know him, and have seen him."

John 14:1-7

Day Eighteen: The Way

This short passage is often read at funerals. Jesus has just washed the disciples' feet. There is an atmosphere of foreboding in the room as he begins to talk to them about the path ahead, which would lead to the cross the next day. "Do not let your hearts be troubled. Believe in God, believe also in me," he says. I have read those words many times, looking at the troubled faces in the front pews of a funeral, as people try to come to terms with the loss of a loved one and wonder what the future holds.

"You know the way to the place where I am going," says Jesus. This is too much for Thomas: "Lord, we don't know where you are going, so how can we know the way?" he asks in exasperation. "I am the way..." says Jesus.

That famous claim of Jesus to be the way, the truth and the life is often taken out of context. At root it is not so much a grandiose claim as a word of reassurance: you do know the way because you know me; you don't need to be troubled because I will be here for you. Just as you know me, you will find that you know my Father as well. In our most troubled, uncertain, lost moments, when we cry out in confusion that we don't know the way, Jesus reassures us. "You do know the way: I am the way: believe in me."

Think:

- In what ways is your heart troubled?
- Are you trying to find your own way?
- How might believing that Jesus is the way, the truth and the life help?
- Can you offer the things that trouble you to him?

Pray:

Lord Jesus
You are the way: help me to follow.
You are the truth: help me to believe.
You are the life: help me to live it.
I offer you my fears for today
And my concerns about tomorrow.
I know that in the Father's house there are many rooms.
I know there is one for me.
I put my trust in you as my guide, my teacher and my saviour,
So that my heart will not be troubled
And I will not be afraid.

The Stranger Road: Dartmoor, Devon, 2022

They came near to the village where they were going, and he acted like he would go further.

They urged him, saying, "Stay with us, for it is almost evening, and the day is almost over."

He went in to stay with them. When he had sat down at the table with them, he took the bread and gave thanks. Breaking it, he gave it to them. Their eyes were opened and they recognised him, then he vanished out of their sight. They said to one another, "Weren't our hearts burning within us, while he spoke to us along the way, and while he opened the Scriptures to us?" They rose up that very hour, returned to Jerusalem, and found the eleven gathered together, and those who were with them, saying, "The Lord is risen indeed, and has appeared to Simon!" They related the things that happened along the way, and how he was recognised by them in the breaking of the bread.

Luke 24:28-35

Day Nineteen: Encountering Jesus

When the disciples recognised Jesus in the "Road to Emmaus" account and he had disappeared from their sight, they were left asking each other, "Were not our hearts burning within us as he talked with us along the road?" They realised they should have known who it was because of this inner sense of excitement and conviction, but it was only on reflection that they could see it. They went racing back down the road to tell the other disciples what they had seen, only to be told that they had seen him too.

There is a Jesuit practice called "Examen", which involves a prayerful reflection on the events of the day in order to detect God's presence and discern God's direction. It is a good thing to think back over the day: the people we have met and the things that have happened, and ask, "Where was God in that? Where have I heard God's voice today? What have I learned? Where have I been closest to Jesus? When was my heart burning within me?"

One Jesuit writer compares this practice with "Rummaging around in a desk drawer for something you know must be there." Jesus is walking beside us on the road, but, because of our preoccupation with the mundane business of living, it is so easy to miss the signs of his presence. His signature is to be found everywhere: from a kind word to a cloud formation and most of all in that tell-tale burning feeling in our hearts.

Think:

- Where might you have encountered Jesus in the last few days?
- What were the tell-tale signs?
- What are the barriers to recognising Jesus?
- How can they be overcome?

Pray:

Lord Jesus,
Every day you are there,
Walking with me along the road.
But I am so caught up in myself:
My thoughts, my feelings, my preoccupations,
That even when my heart is burning, I take no notice.
Lord, open my eyes in the breaking of the bread
So that I can know what I have always known:
That even when the way is hard
You are the resurrection and the life.

Mystical Mushroom: The Garden House, Devon, 2022

On the next day, he was determined to go out into Galilee, and he found Philip. Jesus said to him, "Follow me."

Now Philip was from Bethsaida, of the city of Andrew and Peter. Philip found Nathanael, and said to him, "We have found him, of whom Moses in the law, and the prophets, wrote: Jesus of Nazareth, the son of Joseph."

Nathanael said to him, "Can any good thing come out of Nazareth?"

Philip said to him, "Come and see." Jesus saw Nathanael coming to him, and said about him, "Behold, an Israelite indeed, in whom is no deceit!"

Nathanael said to him, "How do you know me?"

Jesus answered him, "Before Philip called you, when you were under the fig tree, I saw you."

Nathanael answered him, "Rabbi, you are the Son of God! You are King of Israel!"

Jesus answered him, "Because I told you, 'I saw you underneath the fig tree,' do you believe? You will see greater things than these!"

John 1:43-50

Day Twenty: The Ordinary As Extraordinary

"Can anything good come out of Nazareth?" asks Nathaniel. I went to Nazareth a few years ago and I have to say I could see what he meant. If it weren't for the fact that Jesus had lived there, I don't think there would be a big tourist trade: it had a sad, down-at-heel feel to it. Yet by God's providence this is where Jesus spent most of his life.

There are plenty of places you could substitute for Nazareth in Nathaniel's question: places which epitomise drab, boring conformity. Our new estates, which are springing up all over the country, bring to mind the 1960s folk song about little boxes on the hillside: all made out of ticky-tacky and all looking just the same. Yet these little boxes are filled with people who have their own lives: people who God loves.

By his life on earth as a carpenter's son Jesus hallowed the ordinary. There's no such thing as a dull town because in God's eyes there is no such thing as a dull person. If Jesus had lived in some exotic location he would have been more remote, but he lived in Nazareth which was a quiet little provincial place where nothing much happened... until it did. I think Nathaniel may have felt a little foolish when he met Jesus, and his experience should remind us to expect good things in ordinary places.

Think:

- What places can you think of that you could substitute for Nazareth?
- Can you imagine Jesus coming from there?
- What about where you come from?
- Can you be dismissive of people or places as Nathaniel was?
- What can you do to change that?

Pray:

Lord Jesus,
You were always most at home with ordinary people.
You were always most comfortable in ordinary places
You grew up in an ordinary home.
Yet your presence made each one extraordinary.
Lord, I am ordinary:
You are at home in my home
Because I am there.
Yet your presence makes everything
Extraordinary,
Exceptional,
Unique.
Lord Jesus, you are welcome here.

Light Hath No Boundaries: Fresnes-Sur-Apance, France, 2016

83

Doesn't wisdom cry out?
  Doesn't understanding raise her voice?

"Yahweh possessed me in the beginning of his work,
  before his deeds of old.

I was set up from everlasting, from the beginning,
  before the earth existed.

When there were no depths, I was born,
  when there were no springs abounding with water.

Before the mountains were settled in place,
  before the hills, I was born;

while as yet he had not made the earth, nor the fields,
  nor the beginning of the dust of the world.

When he established the heavens, I was there.
  When he set a circle on the surface of the deep,

when he established the clouds above,
  when the springs of the deep became strong,

when he gave to the sea its boundary,
  that the waters should not violate his commandment,
  when he marked out the foundations of the earth."

Proverbs 8:1; 22-29

Day Twenty-One: Before the Beginning

You will be glad to know that the age-old problem of the chicken and the egg has been solved. The egg came first. "Ah, so where did the egg come from?" you must be asking, but think about it like this. Everything evolved from something else, so the first chicken must have emerged from an egg laid by something that wasn't a chicken. The egg came first: problem solved.

The Bible sometimes talks about pre-existence. Wisdom in Proverbs declares that God created her before the earth was made. Paul in Colossians says that Jesus is "before all things," and in him all things were created. John begins his gospel with the famous words "In the beginning was the Word."

This goes deeper than the chicken and the egg. If we simply say that God came first, then it is natural to ask, "Where did God come from then?" Christianity, like other world religions, wants to make a bigger claim about God. We want to say that God is the one in whom we live and move and have our being. God is before all things: not just as the first, the origin, but the ground of all things: the one who makes sense of all things, the one who has always been, who makes possible the very idea of beginnings and endings, the one we experience in time but who is essentially timeless. If you can get your head around that then chickens and eggs start to look very straightforward.

Think:

- *Where were you before you were born?*
- *What difference does it make to our faith that Jesus was with God in the beginning?*
- *If a child asked you "Where did I come from?" what would you say?*

Pray:

Lord God,
Even before I was born you knew me.
When I was still being formed in secret
you saw me and loved me.
I have always been a part of your plan for the world
And I always will be:
Even to the end of time.
You have known my days from the beginning
And you know what lies ahead for me.
I have come from you,
And I am on my journey back to you.
You walk beside me
And you wait for me.
Thank you.

Infinity: Mill Bay Cove, Devon, 2020

After these things, Jesus went away to the other side of the Sea of Galilee, which is also called the Sea of Tiberias. A great multitude followed him, because they saw his signs which he did on those who were sick. Jesus went up into the mountain, and he sat there with his disciples. Now the Passover, the feast of the Jews, was at hand. Jesus therefore lifting up his eyes, and seeing that a great multitude was coming to him, said to Philip, "Where are we to buy bread, that these may eat?" He said this to test him, for he himself knew what he would do.

Philip answered him, "Two hundred denarii worth of bread is not sufficient for them, that every one of them may receive a little." One of his disciples, Andrew, Simon Peter's brother, said to him, "There is a boy here who has five barley loaves and two fish, but what are these among so many?"

Jesus said, "Have the people sit down." Now there was much grass in that place. So the men sat down, in number about five thousand. Jesus took the loaves; and having given thanks, he distributed to the disciples, and the disciples to those who were sitting down; likewise also of the fish as much as they desired. When they were filled, he said to his disciples, "Gather up the broken pieces which are left over, that nothing be lost." So they gathered them up, and filled twelve baskets with broken pieces from the five barley loaves, which were left over by those who had eaten. When therefore the people saw the sign which Jesus did, they said, "This is truly the prophet who comes into the world." Jesus therefore, perceiving that they were about to come and take him by force to make him king, withdrew again to the mountain by himself.

John 6:1-15

Day Twenty-Two: Miracles

People who have trouble believing in miracles will sometimes try to explain them away. One theory about the feeding of the 5000 is the "lunchbox theory". According to this, the crowd were so inspired by seeing the small boy offer his five loaves and two fish to Jesus that they all got their packed lunches out and shared them with each other. As everyone who has ever been to a "bring and share" meal knows there is always food left over.

I don't think I buy that one. This miracle is reported in all four Gospels. It seems to have been a major part of Jesus' popular appeal. The crowd are astonished at what has happened, and soon after you have people who weren't there coming to Jesus and effectively asking him to do it again. "What sign do you do? Our fathers ate manna in the wilderness…"

Why would we want to limit Jesus in our imagination so that he could only do what we could do? In fact, perhaps the problem lies in the poverty of our imagination. Because we have so small a vision of God, our expectation is similarly limited. If we had a big vision, we would expect bigger things. As Paul says in the letter to the Ephesians, "Now to him who is able to do immeasurably more than we can ask or imagine: to him be glory in the church and in Christ Jesus for ever and ever. Amen."

Think:

- *How easy do you find it to believe the miracle stories in the Bible? Why?*
- *Do you feel able to pray for miracles?*
- *Why do you think this miracle had such an impact on the people who were there?*
- *What does it say to us about God?*

Pray:

Lord God,
I know in my head
that there are no limits to your power:
that all things are possible for you.
But I find it hard to believe in my heart
And my prayers are small.
You are not limited by what I can imagine.
You can do immeasurably more.
So I want to pray big prayers.
And even if I do not see miracles
I will still ask for them
Because that is what you told us to do.
I will ask, seek and knock
Until the door is opened.

Sacred Sea: Tintagel, Cornwall, 2016

Therefore Jesus perceived that they wanted to ask him, and he said to them, "Do you inquire among yourselves concerning this, that I said, 'A little while, and you won't see me, and again a little while, and you will see me?' Most certainly I tell you that you will weep and lament, but the world will rejoice. You will be sorrowful, but your sorrow will be turned into joy. A woman, when she gives birth, has sorrow because her time has come. But when she has delivered the child, she doesn't remember the anguish any more, for the joy that a human being is born into the world. Therefore you now have sorrow, but I will see you again, and your heart will rejoice, and no one will take your joy away from you.

"In that day you will ask me no questions. Most certainly I tell you, whatever you may ask of the Father in my name, he will give it to you. Until now, you have asked nothing in my name. Ask, and you will receive, that your joy may be made full. I have spoken these things to you in figures of speech. But the time is coming when I will no more speak to you in figures of speech, but will tell you plainly about the Father. In that day you will ask in my name; and I don't say to you that I will pray to the Father for you, for the Father himself loves you, because you have loved me, and have believed that I came from God. I came from the Father, and have come into the world. Again, I leave the world, and go to the Father."

John 16:19-28

Day Twenty-Three: Heavenly Approval

Rocket Man is a musical about the life of Elton John. The film covers Elton's rise to fame and his struggles with drink, drugs and sexuality. He apparently had a very difficult relationship with his father, who found it impossible to show him any affection. "Are you going to hug me?" asks the five-year-old Elton. "Don't be so soft," says his father.

Towards the end of the film there is a very touching moment when [spoiler alert!] the adult Elton John, having done battle with his demons and emerged on the other side of rehab, has a vision of his five-year-old self. "Are you going to hug me?" asks the boy and Elton kneels and takes him in his arms. Not a dry eye in the house. Elton John has now been free from drink and drugs for over 25 years: he has come to terms with who he is.

So much anguish has at its root a craving for our father's approval: that longing for a hug which means that someone is proud of us and will be there for us no matter what. When it is withheld, people will burn down cities in search of it. Earthly fathers are never perfect, but all of us have an idea of what a perfect father would be like. "On that day,' said Jesus, "You will ask in my name. I am not saying that I will ask the Father on your behalf. For the Father Himself loves you."

Think:

- *How much of what you do is in search of approval?*
- *Whose approval are you seeking? Why?*
- *Can you believe that God approves of you?*
- *What did Jesus mean when he said, "The Father himself loves you"?*

Pray:

Heavenly Father
You know all things
And yet you love me for what I am.
I can make you sad, even angry,
But that relationship cannot be broken,
And you are sad and angry only because
You want the very best for me.
I want to live in that knowledge.
I want to make you proud
I want to be your child:
And an heir of the kingdom.
I put aside my need for human approval
And I rejoice that the Father himself loves me.

Innocence: Coope Farm, Devon, 2015

He called to himself his twelve disciples, and gave them authority over unclean spirits, to cast them out, and to heal every disease and every sickness. Now the names of the twelve apostles are these. The first, Simon, who is called Peter; Andrew, his brother; James the son of Zebedee; John, his brother; Philip; Bartholomew; Thomas; Matthew the tax collector; James the son of Alphaeus; Lebbaeus, who was also called Thaddaeus; Simon the Zealot; and Judas Iscariot, who also betrayed him.

Jesus sent these twelve out and commanded them, saying, "Don't go among the Gentiles, and don't enter into any city of the Samaritans. Rather, go to the lost sheep of the house of Israel. As you go, preach, saying, 'The Kingdom of Heaven is at hand!' Heal the sick, cleanse the lepers, and cast out demons. Freely you received, so freely give. Don't take any gold, silver, or brass in your money belts. Take no bag for your journey, neither two coats, nor sandals, nor staff: for the labourer is worthy of his food. Into whatever city or village you enter, find out who in it is worthy, and stay there until you go on. As you enter into the household, greet it. If the household is worthy, let your peace come on it, but if it isn't worthy, let your peace return to you. Whoever doesn't receive you or hear your words, as you go out of that house or that city, shake the dust off your feet. Most certainly I tell you, it will be more tolerable for the land of Sodom and Gomorrah in the day of judgment than for that city. "Behold, I send you out as sheep among wolves. Therefore be wise as serpents and harmless as doves. But beware of men, for they will deliver you up to councils, and in their synagogues they will scourge you. Yes, and you will be brought before governors and kings for my sake, for a testimony to them and to the nations. But when they deliver you up, don't be anxious how or what you will say, for it will be given you in that hour what you will say. For it is not you who speak, but the Spirit of your Father who speaks in you.

Matthew 10:1-20

Day Twenty-Four: Strong Sheep

"I am sending you out as sheep among wolves," says Jesus as he sends out the disciples. "Therefore be as wise as serpents and innocent as doves."

Snakes do not have a good press in the Bible, and it is interesting to see Jesus advocating imitating one. The difference between wisdom and cunning is only in its purpose. "For the children of this age are more shrewd in dealing with their own generation than are the children of light," Jesus says at the end of the parable known as the "dishonest manager". Innocence does not have to mean naivety: we need to approach the world with our eyes wide open; we need to be aware of how things work.

But the other side of the saying is vital. It is all too easy to get drawn into playing the game by the world's rules, and the history of the church has far too many examples of this, where innocence has been exchanged for power and influence.

The challenge for us as Christians is to accept that we are sheep in the midst of wolves, and therefore to seek to be wise to the dangers while at the same time maintaining our integrity. It is not easy, but if you read the story, you will see that the disciples came back rejoicing.

Think:

- *What are the "wolves" that surround you? (This may be a hard question, but stay with it)*
- *In what ways might you need to "wise up" to the world around?*
- *How can you do that while maintaining your integrity?*

Pray:

Lord, I want to be as wise as a serpent:
To see the danger and avoid it,
To have my eyes open to the ways of the world.
And I want to be as innocent as a dove:
To be in the world without being corrupted by it,
And to stay true to myself and to you.
Lord, I am a sheep among wolves
But you are the Good Shepherd:
Your rod and your staff are my protection
When danger threatens you are there.
So where you send me, I will go,
Venturing into the unknown,
Trusting you to keep me safe.

Lamb: Dartmoor, Devon, 2022

Immediately Jesus made the disciples get into the boat and go ahead of him to the other side, while he sent the multitudes away. After he had sent the multitudes away, he went up into the mountain by himself to pray. When evening had come, he was there alone. But the boat was now in the middle of the sea, distressed by the waves, for the wind was contrary. In the fourth watch of the night, Jesus came to them, walking on the sea. When the disciples saw him walking on the sea, they were troubled, saying, "It's a ghost!" and they cried out for fear. But immediately Jesus spoke to them, saying, "Cheer up! It is I! Don't be afraid."

Peter answered him and said, "Lord, if it is you, command me to come to you on the waters."

He said, "Come!"

Peter stepped down from the boat and walked on the waters to come to Jesus. But when he saw that the wind was strong, he was afraid, and beginning to sink, he cried out, saying, "Lord, save me!" Immediately

Jesus stretched out his hand, took hold of him, and said to him, "You of little faith, why did you doubt?"

When they got up into the boat, the wind ceased. Those who were in the boat came and worshiped him, saying, "You are truly the Son of God!"

Matthew 14:22-33

Day Twenty-Five: Stepping Out In Faith

We've all seen the cartoons where a character runs over a cliff edge and hangs for a moment in the air, arms and legs whirling. Then they realise where they are, and gravity takes over. Fortunately in the cartoon world they always survive. It's funny because it relates to our experience: sometimes it can feel as if we are holding things together by sheer will power and if we stop to think, even for a moment, we will plunge downwards.

In the passage we have just read, the disciples see Jesus walking on the water, and Peter, with commendable courage, gets out of the boat and starts to walk towards him. Then he notices the wind and the waves and immediately he starts to sink. Jesus reaches out and takes his hand. "Where is your faith?" he asks.

When someone freezes with panic on a rock climb the instructor will say to them "Look at me." The instructor can't get them out of the situation: they must do it themselves, but first they must recover their confidence and self-belief, and the best way to do that is to look into the eyes of someone who believes in them. You can see where this is going. We need to rediscover our self-belief; to take our eyes off the wind and the waves and fix them on Jesus. We can't walk on water, but whatever we face, we can get through with him.

Think:

- *What made Peter get out of the boat?*
- *Why did he start to sink?*
- *Which parts of the story can you identify with?*
- *Where are your eyes fixed now?*

Pray:

Lord Jesus,
My self-belief is low.
If I were to get out of the boat,
I would sink like a stone.
But you say, "Look at me."
Lord, I am still in the boat,
But with one foot over the side,
And you say "Come."
I don't know if I dare to do that,
But I will try to hold your gaze:
Then maybe I will find myself
Walking towards you.

Walk These Waters: Sea of Galilee, Israel, 2022

"Again, the Kingdom of Heaven is like a dragnet that was cast into the sea and gathered some fish of every kind, which, when it was filled, fishermen drew up on the beach. They sat down and gathered the good into containers, but the bad they threw away. So will it be in the end of the world. The angels will come and separate the wicked from among the righteous, and will cast them into the furnace of fire. There will be weeping and gnashing of teeth." Jesus said to them, "Have you understood all these things?"

They answered him, "Yes, Lord."

He said to them, "Therefore every scribe who has been made a disciple in the Kingdom of Heaven is like a man who is a householder, who brings out of his treasure new and old things." When Jesus had finished these parables, he departed from there. Coming into his own country, he taught them in their synagogue, so that they were astonished and said, "Where did this man get this wisdom and these mighty works? Isn't this the carpenter's son? Isn't his mother called Mary, and his brothers James, Joses, Simon, and Judas? Aren't all of his sisters with us? Where then did this man get all of these things?" They were offended by him.

But Jesus said to them, "A prophet is not without honour, except in his own country and in his own house." He didn't do many mighty works there because of their unbelief.

Matthew 13:47-58

Day Twenty-Six: Judging Less

Prejudice is an ugly word. "To make negative assumptions about people on the basis of superficial knowledge without reason or experience." Yet we all do it: we see a young person and we make assumptions based on their age, the same with an old person or a smart person or a dirty person. Something goes on in our head which we inherit from our ancestors and was designed to keep us safe: "Is this person dangerous?" It has become a habit: "Is this my kind of person?"

The people of Jesus' hometown did the same with him. They couldn't see past the fact that he was the carpenters' son. He wasn't a rabbi: he was the son of Mary and the brother of James. He was a local lad, they knew all about him: who did he think he was, preaching and teaching and healing? Where did he get all this? As a result, the Bible says he was able to do no great work there and he was surprised at their unbelief.

So many of our beliefs about people, even about great ideas, are based on the flimsiest of experience or evidence. That is natural in itself: we can't know everything, but we do need to be very distrustful of our first assumptions. I have learned over the years that the people I immediately warm to are often not the ones who become friends; the people who I am not so sure about sometimes turn up trumps. We can't help our prejudices, but we can learn not to be ruled by them, and then we won't miss out on the works God wants to do among us.

Think:

- *Are there people or groups of people you tend to dismiss? (Think age, background, accent, clothes, voting habits, as well as race, gender etc.)*
- *Where does this judgement come from?*
- *What would need to happen for you to be less judgemental?*
- *Is there one practical step you could take towards that goal?*

Pray:

Lord, there are people I like,
And people I don't:
People I trust
And people I don't:
People who are my kind of people
And people who aren't.
But it's not right for me to judge
Who to rule in and who to rule out,
Who to draw close and who to push away.
I want to see people with your eyes,
Listen with your ears,
Touch with your hands.
I want to be the carpenter's child
In my hometown.

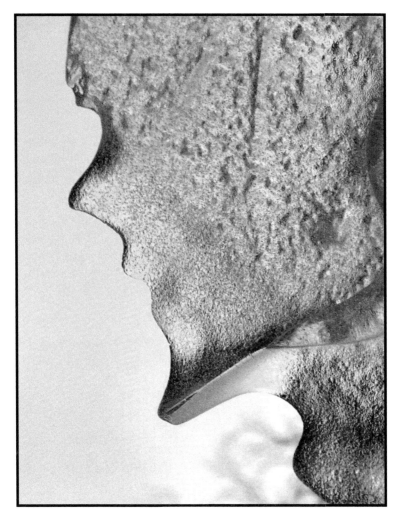

Ice Face: Dartmoor, Devon, 2015

Blessed be the God and Father of our Lord Jesus Christ, who has blessed us with every spiritual blessing in the heavenly places in Christ, even as he chose us in him before the foundation of the world, that we would be holy and without defect before him in love, having predestined us for adoption as children through Jesus Christ to himself, according to the good pleasure of his desire, to the praise of the glory of his grace, by which he freely gave us favour in the Beloved, in whom we have our redemption through his blood, the forgiveness of our trespasses, according to the riches of his grace, which he made to abound toward us in all wisdom and prudence, making known to us the mystery of his will, according to his good pleasure which he purposed in him.

Ephesians 1:3-9

Day Twenty-Seven: Straying From The Path

Winnie the Pooh's friend, Piglet, lived in a house next to a sign which said, "Trespassers Will", which he believed to be short for "Trespassers William", who he understood to be his grandfather. It is a grown-up joke in a children's book: we have all seen the forbidding signs on private ground threatening prosecution if you stray from the path. It's an empty threat, of course: trespass is a civil offence which can not be prosecuted.

We use the word "trespasses" most often in the Lord's Prayer. In more modern versions, it is changed to "sins" to make it more understandable, but I like the old phrase better. Straying from the path onto forbidden ground is a good description of what it means to sin and captures the fact that it is not just about doing wrong things it is also about ending up in wrong places.

"In him we have redemption through his blood, the redemption of our trespasses through the riches of his grace that he lavished upon us…" says St Paul in the passage from Ephesians set for today. "Sin" has so many unhelpful associations that it has almost lost its meaning, but the idea of wandering from the path and being brought back to where we should be is a helpful image for me. The sign is not so much "Trespassers will be prosecuted" as "Trespassers can be redeemed".

Think:

- *About these words and what they mean to you:*
- *Trespasses / sins*
- *Redemption*
- *Grace*
- *If you had to explain their meaning to someone who hadn't heard them before, what would you say?*

Pray:

Lord, I often stray from the path
To places I am not supposed to go.
But you are the Good Shepherd:
You come looking for me and bring me back.
You do not prosecute,
Instead you redeem.
As you have forgiven my wanderings
So I forgive those who have strayed onto my territory.
This is what you command
And this is what I will do
Because you have redeemed me
Through the riches of your grace.

This Path: Kingswear, Devon, 2020

It shall happen, if you shall listen diligently to Yahweh your God's voice, to observe to do all his commandments which I command you today, that Yahweh your God will set you high above all the nations of the earth. All these blessings will come upon you, and overtake you, if you listen to Yahweh your God's voice. You shall be blessed in the city, and you shall be blessed in the field. You shall be blessed in the fruit of your body, the fruit of your ground, the fruit of your animals, the increase of your livestock, and the young of your flock. Your basket and your kneading trough shall be blessed. You shall be blessed when you come in, and you shall be blessed when you go out. Yahweh will cause your enemies who rise up against you to be struck before you. They will come out against you one way, and will flee before you seven ways. Yahweh will command the blessing on you in your barns, and in all that you put your hand to. He will bless you in the land which Yahweh your God gives you. Yahweh will establish you for a holy people to himself, as he has sworn to you, if you shall keep the commandments of Yahweh your God, and walk in his ways. All the peoples of the earth shall see that you are called by Yahweh's name, and they will be afraid of you. Yahweh will grant you abundant prosperity in the fruit of your body, in the fruit of your livestock, and in the fruit of your ground, in the land which Yahweh swore to your fathers to give you. Yahweh will open to you his good treasure in the sky, to give the rain of your land in its season, and to bless all the work of your hand. You will lend to many nations, and you will not borrow. Yahweh will make you the head, and not the tail. You will be above only, and you will not be beneath, if you listen to the commandments of Yahweh your God which I command you today, to observe and to do, and shall not turn away from any of the words which I command you today, to the right hand or to the left, to go after other gods to serve them.

Deuteronomy 28:1-14

Day Twenty-Eight: His Will Be Done

There is a strong connection in the Bible between blessing and obedience. The people of the Old Testament were told time and again that if they wanted to prosper in the land God was giving them, they would need to be faithful to the commands they were being given as well. When things went badly, it was made clear to them that it was because they had strayed from the path. This sort of teaching is easily distorted. "Give money to the church and God will give you back ten times more." "If bad things have happened to you, it must be because you deserve it." From Job's comforters to modern TV evangelists, this simple idea has been misunderstood and exploited for many centuries.

I once met a Devon farmer who told me that the turning point in his life was the moment he realised that God was a better farmer than he was. He began to commit every day's work to God in prayer. His farm went from just about surviving to a thriving business, which was not only making money but serving local people. He didn't see it as a reward: it was just that he was centred in the right place, and because his life was sorted, the farm began to sort itself around him. God blesses those who are obedient because those who are obedient put themselves in a place of blessing: at the centre of God's will for their lives. It is not that we are blessed for being obedient; it's just that blessing and obedience go together.

Think:

- *How near do you feel you are to the centre of God's will for you?*
- *How might you get closer?*
- *Think about different times in your life when you have felt blessed by God: is there anything that connects them?*
- *Are there particular things you are doing you know you should not be, or things you are not doing that you know you should?*

Pray:

Lord, I want to put myself in a place of blessing
And I know that means being obedient
To your commands.
You know my rebellious streak:
You know how hard it is for me
to stay at the heart of your purposes,
how easily I stop trusting you
and start trusting myself.
But that way lies cursing:
Not life, but death.
So I choose
Obedience, Blessing
And Life.

Grazing Grace: Dartmoor, Devon, 2022

Behold, one came to him and said, "Good teacher, what good thing shall I do, that I may have eternal life?"

He said to him, "Why do you call me good? No one is good but one, that is, God. But if you want to enter into life, keep the commandments."

He said to him, "Which ones?"

Jesus said, "'You shall not murder.' 'You shall not commit adultery.' 'You shall not steal.' 'You shall not offer false testimony.' 'Honour your father and your mother.' And, 'You shall love your neighbour as yourself.'

The young man said to him, "All these things I have observed from my youth. What do I still lack?"

Jesus said to him, "If you want to be perfect, go, sell what you have, and give to the poor, and you will have treasure in heaven; and come, follow me." But when the young man heard this, he went away sad, for he was one who had great possessions.

Jesus said to his disciples, "Most certainly I say to you, a rich man will enter into the Kingdom of Heaven with difficulty. Again I tell you, it is easier for a camel to go through a needle's eye than for a rich man to enter into God's Kingdom."

When the disciples heard it, they were exceedingly astonished, saying, "Who then can be saved?"

Looking at them, Jesus said, "With men this is impossible, but with God all things are possible."

Then Peter answered, "Behold, we have left everything and followed you. What then will we have?"

Jesus said to them, "Most certainly I tell you that you who have followed me, in the regeneration when the Son of Man will sit on the throne of his glory, you also will sit on twelve thrones, judging the twelve tribes of Israel. Everyone who has left houses, or brothers, or sisters, or father, or mother, or wife, or children, or lands, for my name's sake, will receive one hundred times, and will inherit eternal life. But many will be last who are first, and first who are last.

Matthew 19:16-30

Day Twenty-Nine: Letting Go Of Money

In October 2021, an investigation dubbed, "The Pandora Papers" gave a glimpse into the way in which the rich and powerful often seek to protect their money. In a world where billions are on the breadline, an elite few stash their cash in offshore accounts and overseas property to avoid paying tax. The news was not unduly surprising: it is what the rich have done for centuries.

"How hard it is for the rich to enter the Kingdom of Heaven!" said Jesus in response to a question from his disciples. A rich young man had just made a genuine enquiry about how to inherit eternal life, but had gone away sad because his wealth had meant more to him. Accumulating wealth is a bid for immortality. In centuries past the rich built mausoleums, now they build space rockets, but it is hard to find eternal life if you are wealthy: harder than it is for a camel to pass through the eye of a needle.

This sobering passage, which is the gospel set for today, is not just about the super-rich though. It is important for all of us to have this insight into the way in which our material possessions lay siege to our soul. We might not be asked to give up everything, but if we were, could we? Jesus could not be clearer: you cannot serve both God and money. He also said that what is impossible for us is possible for God.

Think:

- *If you had been in the rich young man's place, what would you have done?*
- *How much of a grip does money have on your heart?*
- *What might you do about it?*

Pray:

Lord Jesus, I don't want to think about money,
but it is hard because it promises so much.
If I want to be happy
If I want to be secure
If I want to make a mark on the world
I seem to need it.
But you were rich without it
Because you did your Father's will.
So all that I am I give to you,
All that I have I share with you.
This is impossible for me
But all things are possible for God.

Audacious Autumn: Glendalough, Ireland, 2010

119

If I speak with the languages of men and of angels, but don't have love, I have become sounding brass, or a clanging cymbal. If I have the gift of prophecy, and know all mysteries and all knowledge; and if I have all faith, so as to remove mountains, but don't have love, I am nothing. If I give away all my goods to feed the poor, and if I give my body to be burned, but don't have love, it profits me nothing.

Love is patient and is kind. Love doesn't envy. Love doesn't brag, is not proud, doesn't behave itself inappropriately, doesn't seek its own way, is not provoked, takes no account of evil; doesn't rejoice in unrighteousness, but rejoices with the truth; bears all things, believes all things, hopes all things, and endures all things. Love never fails. But where there are prophecies, they will be done away with. Where there are various languages, they will cease. Where there is knowledge, it will be done away with. For we know in part and we prophesy in part; but when that which is complete has come, then that which is partial will be done away with. When I was a child, I spoke as a child, I felt as a child, I thought as a child. Now that I have become a man, I have put away childish things. For now we see in a mirror, dimly, but then face to face. Now I know in part, but then I will know fully, even as I was also fully known. But now faith, hope, and love remain—these three. The greatest of these is love.

1 Corinthians 13:1-13

Day Thirty: Being Truly Known

Who knows you best? You might think the answer is obvious: you do! But I expect, like me, you are sometimes surprised by the way in which other people can tell us things about ourselves that we had never realised. They might not know everything, but they see things from a completely different angle: from the outside. Even though I have lived with myself for over sixty years now, I am still finding things out.

Paul's famous passage about love ends with the words, "Then I shall know fully, even as I am fully known." His life had been turned around by a dazzling encounter on the road to Damascus: he thought he was one thing, he discovered he was another, and his true self had begun to be uncovered. The process was still going on, but he knew for certain that he was "fully known," and that gave him the strength to endure the hardships he was experiencing.

Who you truly are is known only to God. What you see now is like a dim reflection in a cloudy mirror, but one day you will see yourself as God sees you and know God as God knows you. Those words are sometimes missed out when this passage is read at weddings, as if they have nothing to do with what comes before, but the fact is that you are both fully known and fully loved, and one day you will know and love yourself as God knows and loves you. That should be enough to carry you through whatever life may throw at you.

Think:

- *How do you feel about the idea that God knows everything about you?*
- *What are you discovering about yourself at the moment?*
- *What does that suggest might still be discovered?*

Pray:

Lord God,
My vision is clouded and dim.
I understand so little about the world, myself and you.
The little I know shrinks to nothing
Beside what I do not know.
But you know all things
And one day I will know all things
And understand as I have been understood.
So in that hope I stand
And I accept this temporary blindness,
Knowing that one day
I will see your face.

Enchanted Window: Abbey House, Glastonbury, 2015

Now while the multitude pressed on him and heard the word of God, he was standing by the lake of Gennesaret. He saw two boats standing by the lake, but the fishermen had gone out of them, and were washing their nets. He entered into one of the boats, which was Simon's, and asked him to put out a little from the land. He sat down and taught the multitudes from the boat. When he had finished speaking, he said to Simon, "Put out into the deep, and let down your nets for a catch."

Simon answered him, "Master, we worked all night, and took nothing; but at your word I will let down the net." When they had done this, they caught a great multitude of fish, and their net was breaking. They beckoned to their partners in the other boat, that they should come and help them. They came, and filled both boats, so that they began to sink. But Simon Peter, when he saw it, fell down at Jesus' knees, saying, "Depart from me, for I am a sinful man, Lord." For he was amazed, and all who were with him, at the catch of fish which they had caught; and so also were James and John, sons of Zebedee, who were partners with Simon.

Jesus said to Simon, "Don't be afraid. From now on you will be catching people alive."

When they had brought their boats to land, they left everything, and followed him.

Luke 5:1-11

Day Thirty-One: Fishing With Faith

"Master, we have toiled all night and caught nothing," says Peter. "Yet if you say so, we will lower our nets."

Fishing has always been hard, demanding work, and in days before winches, when everything had to be done by hand, hauling wet nets over the side of a boat must have been back breaking. After a fruitless night of toil, the men were tired and hungry, with nothing to feed their families. But their willingness to give it one more go if Jesus said so was rewarded with so many fish that the nets began to break. "From now on you will be catching people," said Jesus.

How's the fishing been in your part of the lake recently? We might well be feeling that we have worked hard and caught very little. Our churches lower the nets on Sunday, but the fish are elsewhere: in the park, at home in bed, in the shops, at work. One response might be to move the boat, and, indeed, on a similar occasion, Jesus told the disciples to lower the nets on the other side, but the centre of this story is their willingness to give it another go if he said so.

Week by week we push our little boats out from the shore. Maybe not this Sunday, or next, or the week after, maybe not this initiative or that, but if we are obedient and do not give up, God will provide the catch. All that is asked of us is that we lower our nets one more time.

Think:

- *Are you feeling you have toiled hard and caught little?*
- *What's your response to being asked to give it another go?*
- *"If you say so..." Who do you feel you are working for?*

Pray:

Lord Jesus, fishing is hard work
And I have caught little.
I don't trust my equipment or my skills.
But you call me to catch people
And you said the Kingdom is like a net.
So show me where to fish
Tell me when to lower the nets
And when to haul them in.
If you say so I will keep fishing
And trust you for the outcome.

Lake At Dawn: Sea of Galilee, Israel, 2019

I command you therefore before God and the Lord Jesus Christ, who will judge the living and the dead at his appearing and his Kingdom: preach the word; be urgent in season and out of season; reprove, rebuke, and exhort with all patience and teaching. For the time will come when they will not listen to the sound doctrine, but having itching ears, will heap up for themselves teachers after their own lusts, and will turn away their ears from the truth, and turn away to fables. But you be sober in all things, suffer hardship, do the work of an evangelist, and fulfil your ministry.

For I am already being offered, and the time of my departure has come. I have fought the good fight. I have finished the course. I have kept the faith. From now on, the crown of righteousness is stored up for me, which the Lord, the righteous judge, will give to me on that day; and not to me only, but also to all those who have loved his appearing.

Timothy 4:1-8

Day Thirty-Two: Discerning The Truth

"People in this country have had enough of experts," said Michael Gove in an interview with Sky News in 2016. It was a defensive comment in response to being asked to name an economist in support of his view, but it is remembered because, in a few words, he captured the spirit of the age. People don't like being told what to think. As a society we are in danger of losing the ability to tell the difference between subjective and objective truth: between the genuine authority and the bloke you met in the pub.

"For the time will come when people will not put up with sound doctrine. Instead, to suit their own desires, they will gather around them a great number of teachers to say what their itching ears want to hear," Timothy is warns in our reading. The letter was written two thousand years ago, but it is a commentary on our time. We like to listen to people who agree with us, who tell us what we want to hear.

Wise people don't do that. Wise people listen to those who tell them what they don't want to hear. Wise people sift through the dross to find those golden nuggets of truth. Wise people have the courage to follow the argument wherever it may lead. Wise people listen to those who know more than they do. Wisdom and faith require us to emerge from our safe little bubble and allow the Truth to speak to us.

Think:

- *Where do you get your news from?*
- *Do you tend to look for information that supports views you already hold?*
- *How open are you to the possibility you might be wrong?*
- *What might you do to ensure that you are more exposed to the truth?*

Pray:

Lord, truth is hard.
It makes demands on me,
It dazzles and confuses,
It upturns my comfortable assumptions
And makes me start again.
But because it is hard, I can build with it
And I can build on it.
That is what I want:
A life built on the rock, not the sand.
So when the storms come
And the floods rise
I will be able to stand.

On Rock, Not Sand: Godrevy, Cornwall, 2018

131

Now we command you, brothers, in the name of our Lord Jesus Christ, that you withdraw yourselves from every brother who walks in rebellion, and not after the tradition which they received from us. For you know how you ought to imitate us. For we didn't behave ourselves rebelliously among you, neither did we eat bread from anyone's hand without paying for it, but in labor and travail worked night and day, that we might not burden any of you, not because we don't have the right, but to make ourselves an example to you, that you should imitate us. For even when we were with you, we commanded you this: "If anyone is not willing to work, don't let him eat." For we hear of some who walk among you in rebellion, who don't work at all, but are busybodies. Now those who are that way, we command and exhort in the Lord Jesus Christ, that they work with quietness and eat their own bread.

But you, brothers, don't be weary in doing what is right. 14 If any man doesn't obey our word in this letter, note that man, that you have no company with him, to the end that he may be ashamed.

2 Thessalonians 3:6-14

Day Thirty-Three: Reaping The Harvest

"They say hard work never killed anyone, but I say why take the risk?" said Ronald Reagan in a wonderful little counterpoint to the work ethic on which America was built. He knew that hard work did in fact kill people: not that many years before people had been worked to death on the Burma Railway. In the modern world all too often people were expected to work with little regard for their health and safety.

On the other hand there is dignity in work and indignity in idleness. To make an honest contribution to the society in which you live is good for you as well as the people you are working for. Time and again studies have shown that work is good for our mental and physical health. That is why St Paul reminds his readers how anxious he and his companions were to work their way and not be a burden on the churches they were serving. In fact, he says, the general principle should be that if you don't work you don't eat.

One of the main ways we grow as Christians is by answering the call to be labourers in God's harvest field. It isn't good for us to sit and be idle when there is work to be done, and God honours us by employing us in the family firm. As we put our shoulder to the wheel, so we find strength, dignity and fellowship. This is true whatever age we are: the job may change but the call to play our part is constant. Far from killing us, this work is life-giving.

Think:

- *Are you a worker or spectator in your church?*
- *Do you see yourself as a host or a guest?*
- *What jobs has God given you to do?*
- *Is there something more you would like to do?*
- *Is there something you need to give up to make that possible?*

Pray:

Lord, you said you would
Set me to catch people:
And you call me to be
A labourer in the harvest field.
You want me to know the dignity of work,
The satisfaction of a job well done
You honour me with a role in your kingdom.
But you also call me to rest
And to know that all that is yours is mine.
Lord, I want to work, to rest, to play
To be your disciple.

Poppy: Fresnes-Sur-Apance, France, 2013

However, I consider those things that were gain to me as a loss for Christ. Yes most certainly, and I count all things to be a loss for the excellency of the knowledge of Christ Jesus, my Lord, for whom I suffered the loss of all things, and count them nothing but refuse, that I may gain Christ and be found in him, not having a righteousness of my own, that which is of the law, but that which is through faith in Christ, the righteousness which is from God by faith, that I may know him, and the power of his resurrection, and the fellowship of his sufferings, becoming conformed to his death, if by any means I may attain to the resurrection from the dead. Not that I have already obtained, or am already made perfect; but I press on, that I may take hold of that for which also I was taken hold of by Christ Jesus.

Brothers, I don't regard myself as yet having taken hold, but one thing I do: forgetting the things which are behind, and stretching forward to the things which are before, 14 I press on toward the goal for the prize of the high calling of God in Christ Jesus.

Philippians 3:7-14

Day Thirty Four: Looking Ahead

Are we defined by our past or by our future? I'd never thought to ask that question until I read again that passage from Philippians. "Forgetting what lies behind and straining forward to what lies ahead, I press on towards the goal for the prize of the heavenly call of God in Christ Jesus."

If ever there was a man with a past that defined him it was St Paul. On the one hand, he was an elite member of his community for all the reasons he has outlined a few verses before: a Hebrew born of Hebrews, educated to the highest level by the best teachers in the land. On the other hand, he was the man who had set out to destroy the church, a name that put fear into the hearts of Christians. His past could have weighed him down, but he had thrown it off and was running down the track with his eyes fixed on the finish line.

We cannot afford to carry our past with us, whether it is good or bad. Instead of looking back with sadness and regret we need to steadfastly turn our heads towards the future. We have a heavenly call to be the people we are now and the people we will be by God's grace. What's past is past: good or bad; this is now; this is what counts; this is what defines us.

Think:

- *Do you define yourself by your past?*
- *What do you need to cast off in order to run the next part of the race?*
- *Does "straining forward to what lies ahead" describe your attitude to life?*
- *What do you think of the "prize of the heavenly call of God"?*

Pray:

Lord, I want to run the race that is set before me
With energy and determination:
Not looking over my shoulder to the past,
But fixing my eyes on the destination.
Lord, I know I need to cast off the things I am carrying
But it is hard to do it.
You know my past is not who I am:
You call me to become what I will be.
One day I will pass the line:
For now, I want to run with all my strength.

The Road: South Devon, 2020

Jesus went out, with his disciples, into the villages of Caesarea Philippi. On the way he asked his disciples, "Who do men say that I am?"

They told him, "John the Baptiser, and others say Elijah, but others, one of the prophets."

He said to them, "But who do you say that I am?"

Peter answered, "You are the Christ."

He commanded them that they should tell no one about him. He began to teach them that the Son of Man must suffer many things, and be rejected by the elders, the chief priests, and the scribes, and be killed, and after three days rise again. He spoke to them openly. Peter took him, and began to rebuke him. But he, turning around, and seeing his disciples, rebuked Peter, and said, "Get behind me, Satan! For you have in mind not the things of God, but the things of men."

Mark 8:27-33

Day Thirty-Five: Through The Darkness

This reading features Peter's famous declaration that Jesus was the Messiah, followed by his equally famous failure to see what that meant, resulting in Jesus saying to him: "Get behind me Satan". Peter was inadvertently echoing the Devil's temptation: telling him that the path ahead need not involve suffering when Jesus knew that it did. At this point in the story, with the shadow of the cross falling across the page, Jesus was more vulnerable to temptation than he had ever been, hence the force of his words.

The Bible never promises us that our path will be pain free. Our friends will tell us they are sure everything will be OK: that is the role of friends, but we won't find that kind of reassurance in Scripture. Instead we are told that when suffering happens, God will be with us, that we will not be abandoned, that it will not overwhelm us. In a world where we have come to expect there to be a pill for every ill, that is worth remembering. Stuff happens: good and bad, whether you are a Christian or not.

Jesus did not need the distraction of being told everything would be all right and nor do we. Instead we need the assurance that, whatever life may hold, our lives are in God's hands, and at the end of the path lies a glory we can only begin to grasp. Jesus knew that beyond the cross lay the empty tomb, and so at this pivotal moment in the story, he can set his face towards Jerusalem.

Think:

- *Do you sometimes find yourself inadvertently falling into the role of tempter?*
- *What is the strongest lure for you from what you know to be the right path?*
- *If Jesus asked you "Who do you say I am?" what would you answer?*

Pray:

Lord Jesus
You didn't want to walk the way of the cross:
You prayed that the cup might pass from you.
Yet you accepted your Father's will.
Lord, I don't want a cross.
I just want everything to be fine,
But I know that joys and sorrows
Are scattered along the path
That all of us must tread.
But you are with me
Your rod and your staff comfort me
And beyond the valley of shadow
You have spread a table for me.

Abbey House Eclipse: Abbey House, Glastonbury, 2015

I therefore, the prisoner in the Lord, beg you to walk worthily of the calling with which you were called, with all lowliness and humility, with patience, bearing with one another in love, being eager to keep the unity of the Spirit in the bond of peace. There is one body and one Spirit, even as you also were called in one hope of your calling, one Lord, one faith, one baptism, one God and Father of all, who is over all and through all, and in us all. But to each one of us, the grace was given according to the measure of the gift of Christ. Therefore he says,

"When he ascended on high,
   he led captivity captive,
   and gave gifts to people."

Now this, "He ascended", what is it but that he also first descended into the lower parts of the earth? 10 He who descended is the one who also ascended far above all the heavens, that he might fill all things.

He gave some to be apostles; and some, prophets; and some, evangelists; and some, shepherds and teachers; for the perfecting of the saints, to the work of serving, to the building up of the body of Christ, until we all attain to the unity of the faith and of the knowledge of the Son of God, to a full grown man, to the measure of the stature of the fullness of Christ, that we may no longer be children, tossed back and forth and carried about with every wind of doctrine, by the trickery of men, in craftiness, after the wiles of error; but speaking truth in love, we may grow up in all things into him who is the head, Christ, from whom all the body, being fitted and knit together through that which every joint supplies, according to the working in measure of each individual part, makes the body increase to the building up of itself in love.

Ephesians 4:1-16

Day Thirty-Six: Growing Up In Christ

We have all wanted at different times to tell certain people to just grow up. When adults behave like children it can be very destructive: growing up involves realising that the world does not revolve around you, that you have responsibilities as well as rights, that pleasure must sometimes be deferred, that someone must do the dirty jobs and that life isn't always fair. It involves taking responsibility, shouldering the burden and seeing yourself as part of a bigger picture.

Growing up features in this extract from the Letter to the Ephesians. "Speaking the truth in love we must grow up in every way into him..." Children speak the truth: "Mummy, why is that man so fat?" Growing up involves speaking the truth in love: recognising that the truth which will set us free is also sharper than a two-edged sword and needs to be handled with skill and care.

Our aim as Christians is to grow up into Christ, becoming just a little more like him each day. It is impossible to have that aim and to be taken up with the childish squabbles that so often mar the life of our communities.

The more we can grow up into him, the more we will be able to take on board his teaching that we must become like little children to enter the kingdom. As we put childish ways behind us, so we can become more childlike in our trust in our Heavenly Father as we grow up into him.

Think:

- *What childish behaviour have you experienced recently?*
- *Are you guilty of it at all? What drives that in you?*
- *What would "growing up" involve for you?*

Pray:

Lord, you call me to grow up
To put childish ways behind
And to face the world as an adult.
So I offer you my self-centredness,
My laziness, my tantrums,
my refusal to take responsibility.
Give me a job instead.
May I speak the truth
But may I speak it in love,
Knowing that the truth can hurt
So I can be a grown up
Because I have grown up into you.

Reflection: Rosemoor Gardens, Devon, 2016

147

In the beginning was the Word, and the Word was with God, and the Word was God. The same was in the beginning with God. All things were made through him. Without him, nothing was made that has been made. In him was life, and the life was the light of men. The light shines in the darkness, and the darkness hasn't overcome it. There came a man, sent from God, whose name was John. The same came as a witness, that he might testify about the light, that all might believe through him. He was not the light, but was sent that he might testify about the light. The true light that enlightens everyone was coming into the world.

He was in the world, and the world was made through him, and the world didn't recognise him. He came to his own, and those who were his own didn't receive him. But as many as received him, to them he gave the right to become God's children, to those who believe in his name: who were born not of blood, nor of the will of the flesh, nor of the will of man, but of God. The Word became flesh, and lived among us. We saw his glory, such glory as of the one and only Son of the Father, full of grace and truth.

John 1:1-14

Day Thirty-Seven: God's True Image

A friend of mine, who had a great influence on my life, has recently died. He was the vicar who married us and who was partly responsible for me being ordained. He once told me that when people said they didn't believe in God he would ask, "What kind of God don't you believe in?" Quite often when they told him he was able to say, "I don't believe in that God either."

Over the centuries people have used the idea of a god or of many gods to explain the unexplainable and to excuse the inexcusable. How did the world begin? God made it. Why is there a crop failure? The Gods are angry with us. Why should I be good? Because God will punish you if you are not. If you trace everything that happens back to some divine being then you end up with an understanding of a God who is capable of being generous but also of being vengeful, even spiteful.

Yet the Bible makes an extraordinary claim about Jesus. "The Word became flesh," says John. "He is the visible image of the invisible God," says St Paul. That man who lived and walked among us, who was capable of being angry at injustice and hypocrisy, also taught us to call God "Father" and told the story of the prodigal son. Here is the absolute against which our wrong understanding of God can be measured and corrected. This is how we know what God we believe in.

Think:

- *What kind of God don't you believe in?*
- *What kind of God do you believe in?*
- *How closely does that match up with the example and teaching of Jesus?*

Pray:

Lord, I have made you in my own image,
I imagine you are other than you are.
But your word became flesh and dwelt among us,
He is the visible image of the invisible God,
He is how I know what you are like.
Lord you are big beyond my imagining,
Powerful beyond my conception
Wise beyond anything I can grasp.
Yet you became someone who could be seen and touched
Someone who laughed and cried, bled and died.
Someone I can know.
Someone I can follow.

Christ, My Lord: Sion Community, Essex, 2022

151

Some indeed preach Christ even out of envy and strife, and some also out of good will. The former insincerely preach Christ from selfish ambition, thinking that they add affliction to my chains; but the latter out of love, knowing that I am appointed for the defence of the Good News.

What does it matter? Only that in every way, whether in pretence or in truth, Christ is proclaimed. I rejoice in this, yes, and will rejoice. For I know that this will turn out to my salvation, through your prayers and the supply of the Spirit of Jesus Christ, according to my earnest expectation and hope, that I will in no way be disappointed, but with all boldness, as always, now also Christ will be magnified in my body, whether by life or by death. For to me to live is Christ, and to die is gain. But if I live on in the flesh, this will bring fruit from my work; yet I don't know what I will choose. But I am hard pressed between the two, having the desire to depart and be with Christ, which is far better. Yet to remain in the flesh is more needful for your sake. Having this confidence, I know that I will remain, yes, and remain with you all for your progress and joy in the faith, that your rejoicing may abound in Christ Jesus in me through my presence with you again.

Philippians 1:15-26

Day Thirty-Eight: Being Mortal, Being Immortal

I suppose there is a time in everyone's life when you have to come to terms with the fact that you won't be around forever. When you are young you kind of assume you are immortal; as you get older you realise that you are not. Every time I take a funeral I think, "One day this will be me". It's a strange thought, especially as it is not a fantasy but a cold hard fact.

As Christians, of course, we have a particular perspective on this: we have a "sure and certain hope", to quote from the funeral service. We don't believe that life ends with the death of our bodies; we believe that death is a gateway to a new life beyond our imagining. This is not a fantasy either: it is based on the life, death and resurrection of our Lord and Saviour, Jesus Christ.

"For me to live is Christ, to die is gain," says St Paul. He goes on to talk about how he is, "Hard pressed between the two": he knows there is still work to be done, but he longs to see the Lord face to face. Perhaps that is the answer: to embrace both mortality and immortality. In this life we have a purpose; in the next we have a place. By God's grace, the later stages of our life can be lived in the ever-increasing glow of eternity.

Think:

- *Do you feel you have faced up to your own mortality?*
- *Do you have a hope for a life beyond the death of your body?*
- *What would it mean for you to embrace your mortality and your immortality?*

Pray:

Lord, you have set eternity in my heart,
Yet in a way that I cannot grasp.
It is hard not to see this life as all there is
And lose my grip on the life to come.
I know my days are numbered
And that you hold that number in your heart
But I would prefer not to think about it:
Not yet at least.
Lord, I want to live this life
In the light of the life to come,
Seeing each day as one step nearer to home
One step nearer to when I shall be fully alive.

Teazle Tease: Rosemoor Gardens, Devon, 2015

155

Isn't this the fast that I have chosen:
  to release the bonds of wickedness,
  to undo the straps of the yoke,
  to let the oppressed go free,
  and that you break every yoke?
Isn't it to distribute your bread to the hungry,
  and that you bring the poor who are cast out to your house?
When you see the naked,
  that you cover him;
  and that you not hide yourself from your own flesh?
Then your light will break out as the morning,
  and your healing will appear quickly;
then your righteousness shall go before you,
  and Yahweh's glory will be your rear guard.
Then you will call, and Yahweh will answer.
  You will cry for help, and he will say, 'Here I am.'
"If you take away from among you the yoke,
  finger pointing,
  and speaking wickedly;
and if you pour out your soul to the hungry,
  and satisfy the afflicted soul,
then your light will rise in darkness,
  and your obscurity will be as the noonday;
and Yahweh will guide you continually,
  satisfy your soul in dry places,
  and make your bones strong.
You will be like a watered garden,
  and like a spring of water
  whose waters don't fail.
Those who will be of you will build the old waste places.
  You will raise up the foundations of many generations.
You will be called Repairer of the Breach,
  Restorer of Paths with Dwellings.

Isaiah 58:6-12

Day Thirty-Nine:
Keeping The Sabbath, Feeding The Hungry

In one of the Old Testament readings set for today from Isaiah 58, there is a strong plea for social justice and a reminder to keep the Sabbath. Both are wrapped in promises. If the people feed the hungry and tend to the afflicted, they will be like a watered garden. If they remember to keep the Sabbath, then they will ride upon the heights of the earth.

There is a connection between the two. The Sabbath is there to prevent exploitation of the earth and of people. If our whole lives are about doing and getting and producing and never about resting, reflecting and enjoying, then we will exhaust the earth and ourselves. If we attune ourselves to God's priorities, then the poor will be looked after and we ourselves will flourish. In the Gospel reading, Jesus breaks this rule in order to keep it: he heals a crippled woman on the Sabbath Day. The religious leaders are outraged, but he points out to them that they water their animals on the Sabbath. The Sabbath is intended to enable healing, not to prevent it.

Try to rediscover that Sabbath principle this week. Seek God's priorities in your attitudes towards others and yourself. Step back in order to discover a way forward. Then, in the words of the prophet, "The Lord will guide you continually and satisfy your needs in parched places and make your bones strong... you shall be called the repairer of the breach, the restorer of streets to live in."

Think:

- *What have you done this week to feed the hungry?*
- *How is God's sabbath principle worked out in your life?*
- *How do these two go together?*

Pray:

Lord, you call me to feed the hungry and keep the sabbath.
It is so easy to ignore both commands:
To think my needs are all that matter
And to make every day much the same.
Lord, there needs to be a sabbath in my life:
I need to take time out:
Not to waste it but to live it,
So that my needs are met, and my bones are strong.
Then I can be a source of strength
And a repairer of the breach
And a restorer of streets to live in.

Balance: St Ives, Cornwall, 2018

Then they arrived at the country of the Gadarenes, which is opposite Galilee. When Jesus stepped ashore, a certain man out of the city who had demons for a long time met him. He wore no clothes, and didn't live in a house, but in the tombs. When he saw Jesus, he cried out, and fell down before him, and with a loud voice said, "What do I have to do with you, Jesus, you Son of the Most High God? I beg you, don't torment me!" For Jesus was commanding the unclean spirit to come out of the man. For the unclean spirit had often seized the man. He was kept under guard, and bound with chains and fetters. Breaking the bonds apart, he was driven by the demon into the desert.

Jesus asked him, "What is your name?"

He said, "Legion," for many demons had entered into him. They begged him that he would not command them to go into the abyss. Now there was there a herd of many pigs feeding on the mountain, and they begged him that he would allow them to enter into those. Then he allowed them. The demons came out of the man, and entered into the pigs, and the herd rushed down the steep bank into the lake, and were drowned. When those who fed them saw what had happened, they fled and told it in the city and in the country. People went out to see what had happened. They came to Jesus and found the man from whom the demons had gone out, sitting at Jesus' feet, clothed and in his right mind; and they were afraid. Those who saw it told them how he who had been possessed by demons was healed. All the people of the surrounding country of the Gadarenes asked him to depart from them, for they were very much afraid. Then he entered into the boat and returned. But the man from whom the demons had gone out begged him that he might go with him, but Jesus sent him away, saying, "Return to your house, and declare what great things God has done for you." He went his way, proclaiming throughout the whole city what great things Jesus had done for him.

Luke 8:26-39

Day Forty: Abiding With Him

One of the very strange aspects of the story of the healing of Legion is that when the people of the region come and find the man who has been terrifying them for years healed and in his right mind, they beg Jesus to go away. You would think that they would have begged him to stay: there must have been many other people in that community who needed healing. Maybe it was because the curing of Legion had cost them a herd of pigs, but I suspect there was a deeper reason.

Legion was an exile amongst the tombs: one of the Gospel accounts says he was chained up. The people had dealt with him in their own way; they had shut him and his disturbing mental illness into a corner so they could get on with their lives. What happened destroyed this carefully built equilibrium and potentially called into question the foundations of their society. Much better to exclude the disturber and try to get back to the way things were.

Jesus is not a comfortable person to have around. If you feel you are only just about holding things together, it is easy to exclude him on the basis that you would rather settle for things as they are than have your cage rattled in the way that he has a habit of doing. But the story of Legion should remind us of the possibilities we might be excluding if we ask him, however politely, to please go away.

Think:

- *Are there times when you ask Jesus to go away?*
- *What is there about your life that Jesus threatens to disturb?*
- *What possibilities might you be excluding?*

Pray:

Lord Jesus, you disturb my peace
But I don't want you to go away,
I want you to stay.
I want to sit at your feet,
clothed and in my right mind,
with all the raging gone.
For that to happen I need you here,
So stay, Lord Jesus:
Abide with me, for the night is falling,
Make yourself known in the breaking of bread.

Light In The Dark: Rosemoor Gardens, Devon, 2022

Note On Photographs

Many of the images used in this book are new, and have never been seen before. A number of others have been previously circulated and marketed through **Mikhal Brandstatter Photography.**

While most of the titles have remained the same, a few have been changed according to the accompanying text.

Some of the photographs may also have been edited for the specific purpose of this book. They may have been cropped differently and/or had the colour and light altered.

The quality of the colour and shade have also been affected by the printing process.

The dates the photographs were taken range from 2007 to 2022.

If you would like to purchase any of these images, you are able to do so - either in their original form or in the ones found in the book.

They can be purchased in a number of media, including prints, cards and canvases.

Please contact Michal if you would like further information and/ or to make a purchase:

mikhal2@gmail.com

Acknowledgements

Michal would like to thank Samson Kambalu, for his kind permission to use her image of his sculpture, ***Antelope***, presently exhibited on the fourth plinth at Trafalgar Square. For the fascinating story of this sculpture and details of his other work and activities, please visit his website:

samsonkambalu.com

The drawing, ***Christ, My Lord***, is by Valerie Dalton, and is displayed at Sion Community:

sioncommunity.org.uk

Stephen would like to thank Gilly Bromilow, Tony Wood and Rob Flexman for their support and input in choosing which material to include in this book.

List of Images

(Copyright Michal Brandstatter)

Printed in Great Britain
by Amazon

18348671R00098